I believe that the Twelve Steps are a mov
our time, in many ways rediscovering tl
power of the gospel. In their reflections,
out the vulnerability, healing, and love
of both Jesus' teaching and the Twelve St
any Christian for whom working the program is a lifeline,
and for any person interested in the honesty, willingness, and
surrender that are at the heart of what founder Bill Wilson
called "a vital spiritual experience."

RICHARD ROHR, *author of numerous books including*
The Divine Dance: The Trinity and Your Transformation

There is something about a good sermon that brings tears
and a chuckle in the same moments. This what I found
myself doing as I read *The Twelve Steps Meet the Gospel*. Often
those of us in recovery fail to see the wisdom and grace
that religious traditions have to offer in our journey. A
good biblical story brings profound truth to all people, but
especially to those of us who have known a low point in life
and need to hear a new hope through recovery. As a person
in recovery myself and also as a pastor who has given many
hundreds of sermons in the recovery community, my only
regret was that I couldn't have been on the other side of the
pulpit to hear these insightful sermons each week. Well
done, Trish and Dick! Well done!

JO CAMPE, *founding Pastor of the Recovery Methodist Church
in St. Paul, MN*

Recovering addicts didn't need M. Scott Peck to tell them "life is difficult." They know it. They recognized how they were powerless over their train-wrecked lives. They came to believe that a Higher Power could restore them to sanity. They turned their lives and wills over to the care of God as they understood God...every day of their lives. The witness Trish and Dick share as members of the "Order of the Wounded" opens for us a path that accepts human woundedness and despair in the context of steps they have taken to live in joy, peace, and freedom. We in the church need their witness.

ROC O'CONNOR, *theologian, composer, and author*
of In the Midst of Our Storms

As an addictions educator, I've spent much of my forty-year career translating the more religious spiritual expressions of twelve-step literature into universal and thus more accessible concepts for myself and the many others I encounter who feel blocked from twelve-step recovery by their religious upbringing, justifiable religious resentments, more scientific/intellectual approaches to life...it's a long list. What a joy it is to realize that Dick Rice and Trish Vanni are providing—especially for "believers" who struggle with addiction—authentic translations of the Christian liturgical year and related Scriptures into more accessible recovery principles. The text Alcoholics Anonymous states on page 87, "Be quick to see where religious people are right. Make use of what they offer." And so you will, through this wonderful collection.

FRED HOLMQUIST, *Director of the Lodge Program at the Hazelden*
Betty Ford Foundation's Dan Anderson Renewal Center
in Center City Minnesota

THE TWELVE STEPS MEET THE GOSPEL

THE TWELVE STEPS MEET THE GOSPEL

REFLECTIONS ON SCRIPTURE
AND STORIES OF HOPE
FOR THOSE IN RECOVERY

DICK RICE
and TRISH VANNI

**TWENTY-THIRD
PUBLICATIONS**
twentythirdpublications.com

TWENTY-THIRD PUBLICATIONS
1 Montauk Avenue, Suite 200, New London, CT 06320
(860) 437-3012 » (800) 321-0411 » www.twentythirdpublications.com

ISBN:978-1-62785-261-6
Library of Congress Catalog Card Number: 2017932939
Printed in the U.S.A.

 A division of Bayard, Inc.

Contents

INTRODUCTION

*Sought through prayer and meditation to improve
our conscious contact with God as we understood Him,
praying only for knowledge of His will for us
and the power to carry that out.*

■ STEP ELEVEN, *Alcoholics Anonymous*

With its bouncy alliteration, "Conscious Contact" might be the most delicious phrase in the Twelve Steps. It describes the dance with God that we in recovery are about. It also sums up the purpose of this book—to share the light that the Scriptures we hear each week shine on the experience of recovery, and to offer a new lens for all readers to see new depth and richness in God's constant message of unconditional love.

Back to "conscious contact" for a moment. Both words begin with the prefix *con*, which means "with" in Latin. The rest of the first word means "knowledge" or "knowing," and the second half of the next word means "touch." This is much more, however, than simply "knowing touch," as when someone touches your elbow. The prefix indicates mutuality, a joined touch and a joined knowledge. We are each knowingly reaching out and touching, even as we are touched.

Furthermore, the initiative is God's. We reach out only in response to the One who has reached out to us. God has spoken to us in every breath, in every moment. Our response is anchored in gratitude and moves to praise and petition and contrition when appropriate.

In *Alcoholics Anonymous*, more commonly called the "Big Book," people in recovery are reminded that religious practice can be a support in recovery. The Chapter "We Agnostics" notes, "We, who have traveled this dubious path, beg you to lay aside prejudice, even against organized religion." In the rhythms and practices of the Christian liturgical year, and in the Scriptures that worship offers, we can find support for countless principles of recovery. With that in mind, this collection of homilies/sermons is a reflection on our conscious contact with God throughout the Christian Church year.

In the chapter on the Twelfth Step, the book *Twelve Steps and Twelve Traditions* asks, "can we bring new purpose and devotion to the religion of our choice?" Doing so has been a great source of hope and strength for our authors in their journey of recovery. In this book, they have attempted to stay in conscious contact with the God of their understanding, with the texts, and with one another, so that you, the reader, might find new ways to be in conscious contact with the Higher Power you embrace, as well.

Advent

"He comes, comes, ever comes...."

■ RABINDRANATH TAGORE

Christians are fond of saying that Advent remembers the coming of Jesus the Christ into history, longs for the coming of Christ in majesty, and celebrates the coming of the Spirit of Christ right here, right now. Both as Christians and as people in recovery, ours is a journey of progress, not perfection. We are always following Christ, always climbing the steps, always waking up without ever arriving until we have completed the journey. And so it is right to say that our Higher Power comes without ever fully arriving in this life and, in response, we journey without fully arriving until we die. As Augustine wrote, "You have made us for yourself and our heart is restless until it rests in you."

Advent is the season that honors that relentless restlessness and so—we hope—do these reflections. (**DR**)

Becoming Light Bearers

*"Therefore, stay awake, for you know neither
the day nor the hour."* ■ MATTHEW 25:13

*Alcoholics Anonymous is a fellowship of men
and women who share their experience, strength and hope
with each other that they may solve their common problem
and help others to recover from alcoholism.*

■ THE PREAMBLE

Advent is a season of waiting, hope, and, as the Scriptures remind us, light breaking into the darkness.

In Jesus' parable about the lamp-bearing virgins who await the bridegroom, we learn a great deal about light: who has it, who doesn't; how light must be tended to keep it burning; why it's important to be watchful and prepared; and the risk we run when we don't have a well-fueled and trimmed source. If we are not watchful, the darkness can engulf us in a moment.

On first read, we might see this parable as the one in which Jesus tells us (among other things) that we shouldn't share! As a mother, I've had ample opportunity to deal with the question of sharing—who's not sharing, who should be sharing, who's getting the better end of the sharing. At first glance, it seems that the "wise" bridesmaids are actually the selfish bridesmaids—they won't take from their own stores to help the others. Of course, this must be too superficial a reading, because so many of Jesus' stories tell us in detailed and even radical ways to give to one another generously. So "don't share" can't possibly be the point of this Advent parable!

Perhaps what it points to is that there are things we possess that, for a range of reasons, we *can't* give to others—as much as we'd like to. There are some essential but intangible things we cannot give to people even when we see their dire need for them. We can't hand people the surrender that the First Step requires. We can't give them serenity or acceptance. We can't hand someone faith or peace as they struggle to embrace the new way of living that the Twelve Steps offer.

These intangibles that we possess well up like an inner fuel source within us from our deep relationship with the divine. Fortunately, while we can't "give," we can tell people how we got these inner stores—we can lay out our "path" so that others may "thoroughly follow" it. In doing this, we are acting much like the wise bridesmaids who told the foolish bridesmaids where to buy the oil they needed.

I remember a day someone very dear to me called to share her grief over her recent miscarriage. She knew that personal experience gives me a particular compassion and understanding around this issue. I would have liked nothing better in that phone call than to be able to hand over the peace and acceptance I have come to know. But I couldn't do that. I couldn't pull from that personal spiritual well and fill her cup, as much as I wanted to do that. But I could be with her and bear light from my own experience as she journeyed.

In so many moments in life, we can have full-enough lamps to be awake and able to come alongside others in their pain. And we can be awake enough to realize when we need to replenish our stores. I can't be there for others if I've run myself empty. Isn't it interesting that the term we use for that utter emptiness is "burned out"? The parable of the "wise and foolish" virgins reminds us that there is something in our Christian life, and in our sharing of the program, that constantly needs to be replenished, lest it burn out. Fortunately, we have an unlimited, utterly generous source. This is the gift of meetings, of our literature, of a good sponsor who knows "our case." In all of these things, God lights our path.

Our journey of recovery is one of moving from darkness to light, with the support of others. We share "our experience, strength and hope with each other," so that others may discover and claim their own experience of healing. The Al-Anon closing says this so well, when it suggests that we each "let the understanding, love, and peace of the program grow in [us] one day at a time." (TV)

God Breaking into Our Story

"So will it be at the coming of the Son of Man. Two men will be out in the field; one will be taken and one will be left. Two women will be grinding meal; one will be taken and one will be left. Therefore, stay awake! For you do not know on which day your Lord will come."

■ MATTHEW 24:38, 40–42

He finds himself in possession of a degree of honesty, tolerance, unselfishness, peace of mind, and love of which he had thought himself quite incapable. What he has received is a free gift, and yet usually, at least in some small part, he has made himself ready to receive it.

■ *Twelve Steps and Twelve Traditions*, P. 107

I've been going to meetings for what we euphemistically call "a few 24s." Some people in my life have scoffed at this, asking with incredulity, "Why are you still going to those meetings?" Well, I go for a lot of reasons. I go to be of service, to give back gifts that were so freely given to me. I go to fill my spiritual well, to remember that there is a God, as I choose to call the Higher Power, and it's not me. And I go to hear the stories.

The stories serve me not because they are entertaining (which they often are) or insightful (although I always take away what I call a "golden nugget") but because they wake me up. They sweep me not into another's reality, but into my own—what I was like, what happened, what it is like now. I see that God is not done with me. That there are still things to learn and things to do. That I had better "stay awake" one day at a time, and remember to give away what I hope to keep.

The stories of Advent speak of darkness and light—light so great that no darkness can overcome it, stories about paths being made straight, about voices crying out, about vulnerable women taking great leaps of faith, about God coming not like a warrior king on a stallion but as a human child, a vulnerable baby born to an oppressed people.

I imagine that there has never been a time when our Advent stories were not important. Humankind has often wandered into the darkness. But our situation today feels particularly heavy. As I listened to the morning news, I heard reports of increased deadly violence in a stressed city neighborhood, fractious name-calling by politicians, heretofore marginalized indigenous people fighting to protect the environment, and a call to address racism in its many insidious faces. I'm in need of Advent. I'm in need of the reminder that this God who loves stories has a few amazing ones still to tell.

Do you remember *Left Behind*, Tim LaHaye's bestselling series about the rapture? One minute the protagonist, Cameron "Buck" Williams, is on a plane; the next minute, half of the passengers are gone, leaving only their clothing. They have been "raptured." I think about that when I think of this passage from Matthew—what's this "one is taken, one will be left" thing? Where's Elizabeth? John? Mary? Simeon? Anna? I'd take any of them, but instead you give us *Left Behind*?

It's important to remember that this interpretation of this Gospel was first developed by Cotton Mather, the Puritan, and popularized by the Plymouth Brethren at the end of the nineteenth century. Before then, the interpretation was precisely the opposite. The words Jesus used—left and taken away—are the same words used when Babylon, Assyria, and Rome invaded Israel, taking away the residents while leaving behind a lucky remnant. For Jesus' listeners, being "taken" would have been incredibly undesirable. Those that are left behind, are in fact, those brought forward into the kingdom. They are working, but they are alert, and their focus is not on the skies but on the earth, on the job that is here and now.

My friend Paul is a real example of this. Years ago, Paul got involved with an organization called "Results" that was working to address global hunger. In a training, Paul learned about something called "oral rehydration therapy," an incredibly simple solution to dysentery, which at the time was killing millions of children around the globe. It entails mixing a small amount of salt and a handful of sugar into some distilled water and feeding the mixture to the suffering.

Paul was really taken by how accessible and simple the solution was. He called his congressman and asked for an appointment. He and five friends showed up with a video that explained the solution. The congressman returned to Washington and worked to pass legislation to fund a worldwide outreach using "oral rehydration therapy." The year following implementation, the numbers of children dying from dysentery dropped literally by the millions.

I don't think for a minute that when he picked up the phone, Paul thought that he could singlehandedly save millions of children. But having seen Paul in action over the years, I notice that he's someone who's awake while he's grinding in the kitchen. The one phone call, that one turn of the grinding wheel, set the rest in motion.

What kind of Advent might we all have if our focus was on the tasks before us, if our focus was on the ways in which God is breaking in to our story, hoping to write some new words through us?

Advent reminds us to remember the story and remember that God made us for it—the story of God breaking in, the story of God engaged with each of us, holding on to us, never letting us go. God comes at an unexpected hour, in unexpected places, in unexpected voices. How well we in the program know this!

And if we remember that, if we remember we were made for the story, we are part of the story, and we have the courage to tell the story, God will be able to use us in ways we can barely imagine. (TV)

Saying "Yes" to God's Will

"Behold, I am the handmaid of the Lord.
May it be done to me according to your word." ■ LUKE 1:38

God, I offer myself to Thee—to build with me
and to do with me as Thou wilt... ■ THE THIRD STEP PRAYER,
Alcoholics Anonymous, PAGE 63

I have had the opportunity as a pilgrim to visit the Church of the Annunciation in Nazareth. The main floor is filled with different countries' tributes to Mary, the Mother of Jesus. But the real action is in the basement, and even below the basement in a sub-level. There sits the first church, today just a small altar with the words across the front of it (in Latin): HERE THE WORD OF GOD BECAME FLESH.

I was absolutely blown away by the realization that here, or at a place close by, God chose to inhabit the body of a woman. It is almost as though, if you and I had arrived five minutes earlier, we might have witnessed Mary and the angel, as God chose to enter human history in the womb of this woman. God chose to come to us as human that we might again come home to God as his children. This is the mystery of the Annunciation, and this is the mystery of Christmas.

The way the author of Luke's gospel is inspired to tell the story, Mary is the least and last that we would expect to be the hostess for God's homecoming. We have been led through centuries of expectation and Scriptures to believe that if God were to visit us humans, it would be to a man who would be in the temple at Jerusalem, offering sacrifice. That was how the birth of John the Baptist was announced to Zechariah just previously in Luke's gospel. But when it came to Jesus, the Son of God, it was to an unimportant woman in a seemingly God-forsaken town of a seemingly God-forsaken people, Nazareth in Galilee. Mary is the *last* one we would expect to be the recipient of God-becoming-human, and yet she is God's choice, not because of anything she is or has done but because God is God and this is how God chooses to come to us.

And because Mary said YES, and because God now is among us as Jesus in human form and in his Spirit in risen form, we now have God among us every time we say YES to God's will and not simply to our own willfulness. Christmas happens every time we take the Third Step and turn our will and our lives over to God—in that choice God is born again into our time and our space. We are not simply preparing to celebrate the Christmas of 2000 years ago or the Christmas that will come forever at the end, but the Christmas that comes every time we make room in our hearts, in our wills, for the Christ to be born. We are the manger, we are the crib right here, right now. Merry Christmas. (DR)

Christmas

I recently had the opportunity to lead an evening on "Twelve-stepping Through the Holidays" for a community of recovering people. Those of us gathered agreed that our major task in recovery through this season is to lower our expectations. God bless, we are an idealistic people with huge expectations, often of both others and ourselves. We so want the perfect White Christmas, the perfect gift given and received, the perfect relationship with the perfect person, the perfect reconciliation and amends. Do you know what? Christmas wasn't that way the first time and it won't be that way this time. It will be what it will be and, if I can lower the bar of world high-jump record expectations and simply pray to remain serene and loving, I might not only survive Christmas, I might actually enjoy it.

And for all of that, let us not be surprised if the Winter Witch of Fear visits us this season. She visited Mary at the Annunciation, and she is liable to be lying in wait for us this season. "Be not afraid," the angel said, noticing how petrified Mary was, realizing she could never win God's favor or even God's love or be deserving, by her own efforts, of that love. God already loved her just as she was, not because of anything Mary had done or not done, but because God is God and God's love is always and everywhere. Mary gradually relaxes into that realization and can finally say, "Behold the handmaid of the Lord. May it be done unto me according to Thy word."

We all know those four paragraphs about *fear* in *Alcoholics Anonymous* (pages 67, 68) and how fear can "steal" our serenity even quicker than a resentment can. This season, when we find ourselves afraid of rejection, of not doing it right, of failure, or of success, may we remember to call on our Higher Power, as "the Big Book" reminds us:

> Perhaps there is a better way—we think so. For we are now on a different basis; the basis of trusting and relying upon God. We trust infinite God rather than our finite selves. We are in the world to play the role God assigns. Just to the extent that we do as we think God would have us, and humbly rely on God, does God enable us to match calamity with serenity. (page 68)

When all was said and done, Mary got beyond her fear. The same can be true this Christmas for you and me. We might not only endure this Christmas, survive this Christmas, we might actually *enjoy* this Christmas as long as we remember to give birth to our recovery. That simply has to come first. Then let us remember to offer ourselves in service to our brothers and sisters. **(DR)**

Love and Acceptance

And he said to them, "Why were you looking for me? Did you not know that I must be in my Father's house?" ■ LUKE 2:41–52

Can we bring the same spirit of love and tolerance into our sometimes deranged family lives that we bring to our A.A. group?
■ STEP TWELVE, *Twelve Steps and Twelve Traditions*

The Nativity paints such a beautiful picture—the Christ child, his two devoted parents, a host of angels, shepherds gathered from their fields. It's humble but perfect in so many ways, and in that silent night, we really can see how Jesus, Mary, and Joseph are the Holy Family.

In contrast, the story of Jesus' adolescent escapades in Jerusalem is not so picture perfect! It's loaded with confusion and distress. It has multiple instances of poor communication. And it is full of human frailty and fear. Because of that, because it is full of the reality of our own experience of being part of a human family, it may be in some ways an even more powerful story about the miracle of the Incarnation than the story of that night in Bethlehem.

The story of Jesus running off to the Temple speaks to us on two levels. On one level, it speaks theologically: it wants to tell us something about God. And on another level, it speaks emotionally: it wants to tell us something crucial about being human.

Can you relate to Mary and Joseph? I have never heard this story without one of my own experiences of misplacing a child coming to mind—it takes my imagination right to the feelings of fear and dread, fury and relief. Can you imagine the conversation between Joseph and Mary when they realized that they had misplaced their child, the mortification as they told the friends and family members with whom they were traveling, the desperation they felt as three days passed and they couldn't find him?

Or maybe you can relate to Jesus. Here is this very curious and independent adolescent: twelve years old, almost a man but not quite. Can we say he was a tad impulsive to wander off on his own without any notice to his parents, a little disregarding of how his choice would affect those around him? Were you like him once? Are you like him now?

There is not a lot in my experience that directly relates to a miraculous birth with legions of angels. But losing track of a precious child or experiencing frustration and anger toward someone who has disappointed me, or feeling misunderstood by parents? That's my world. As people in recovery, many of whom experienced epic dysfunction in our families of origin, we can relate to all those things and more.

So… in the midst of all of this stress and distress, in this story that is just like our lives, where do we see this family's holiness?

I think the holiness is not actually in anything they're doing. In fact, much of what they've done in relationship to one another has been part of the problem. I think the holiness is in who they are willing be for one another. Somehow, despite the hurt and misunderstandings, they are able to move to a place of love and acceptance. Mary, we are told, doesn't understand fully what is going on. She is, however, willing to ponder in her heart how God's will is playing out in this complicated child's life. And Jesus, while surprised and perhaps even disappointed that his parents did not know him better, doesn't defy them, but returns to Nazareth, where, we are told, he was obedient to them, and grew in wisdom and grace.

Once at a dinner with my extended family, one of the members did something quirky bordering on crazy making. Rather than react with irritation, my mother turned to me and said, "You know, honey, the older we get, the more we just become who we are." She said this with a tremendous tone of acceptance. It struck me that it was not just a very wise observation on my mother's part, but an incredibly loving one. What do any of us want more, as we travel through life, than to be loved and accepted for who we are? And what greater gift can we give someone else, than the acceptance we speak of in our serenity prayer?

Our families are sometimes the hardest places to show this, because our expectations are so great and our investment is so high. It's what makes it hard to watch the young people we love make choices we don't agree with or even choices that we respect that seem too bold or daring. And it's what makes it hard for teens and adolescents to accept us in return, when they don't understand us and our rules or expectations.

This challenge of loving acceptance is not solely between parents and children, but in every important relationship. Some of us face it with siblings or friends or colleagues. We encounter it in our faith communities or our Twelve-Step groups. And the challenge of loving acceptance is an issue for the entire human family, as the world becomes more and more connected and yet never seems to become more peaceful. Our *Twelve Steps and Twelve Traditions* ("12 and 12") puts it this way: "Can we bring the same spirit of love and tolerance into our sometimes deranged family lives that we bring to our A.A. group?" The rooms of the program are where we get to practice this new approach to living among others.

In this season that celebrates the miracle of a God who took human form, we declare that God has loved us so fully that he has entered our very reality to share it and to know it, to experience its glory and its messiness, to know our struggles, and to understand. And to permeate everything with grace, so we know that a journey toward love and acceptance is not simply a nice idea, but a real possibility—not just in select locations, but in every place we are found. (TV)

I Am a Child of God

"So you are no longer a slave, but a child of God."
■ GALATIANS 4:4–7

God is the Father, and we are His children.
■ *Alcoholics Anonymous,* PAGE 62

I must admit that I am not much for New Year's resolutions, as I think I once remembered one and kept it until January 19. That was the longest. However, I am all for New Year's *petitions,* à la the Seventh Step. Resolutions are our good idea; petitions are our response to God's invitation. So let us humbly ask God to remove our shortcoming, the shortcoming of not often enough, deeply enough treating ourselves and one another as the children of God that we are. What if this year, by the grace of God, we ate as a child of God, exercised as a child of God, made love as a child of God, worked as a child of God, and spoke with others as if they were also children of God, listened to them as if they also were children of God, worked with them and played with them as if they also were children of God? What a year it could be! A little bit of heaven, a moment in the kingdom wherever we were.

For years I loved going to the Penumbra Theatre's Christmas production of *Black Nativity* in St. Paul, especially because at the end the whole ensemble broke out into "If they ask you who you are, tell them you are a Child of God." They sang the truth. Recovery community, I dare us, as we each go out into this new year—if anyone asks us who we are, I dare us, I *dare us*, to simply and deeply answer: "I am a Child of God."

Happy New Year. **(DR)**

Our Journey and Epiphanies

*And behold, the star that they had seen at its rising preceded them,
until it came and stopped over the place where the child was.*

■ MATTHEW 2:9

*Here and there, once in a while, alcoholics have had what
are called vital spiritual experiences. They appear to be in the nature
of huge emotional displacements and rearrangements. Ideas, emotions
and attitudes which were once the guiding forces of these men are
suddenly cast to one side, and a completely new set of conceptions
and motives begin to dominate them.*

■ CARL JUNG TO BILL W., AS DESCRIBED IN *Alcoholics Anonymous*

In the weeks leading up to Christmas, our sanctuaries rang
with the hymn "O come, O come, Emmanuel." As we sang,
we focused on the Messiah about to be born. Awaiting the
coming of Jesus, our gaze was fixed on December 25th. But
the word Emmanuel, which means "God with us," points not
only to in a moment in time 2000 years ago, or a moment on
the horizon as the year draws to a close, but to every moment
of our lives.

We believe that God is truly with us, and that we can
grow in our conscious contact with that God as we work the
steps. Christians use the word "grace" to describe this reality
of God-presence with us. The Catholic theology of grace is

nothing less than participation in the divine life, a life that animates and touches us directly. The great theologian Karl Rahner, SJ, described grace this way: "Grace is God himself, his communication, in which he gives himself to us as the divinizing loving kindness which is himself."

When we recognize God's presence, God's grace, we have an opportunity to see things clearly, perhaps as we have never seen them before. We might describe these as "aha!" moments. Some people call them epiphanies.

The word epiphany derives from the Greek word *epifania*, which means an appearance, or a becoming manifest. But it's an appearance in the sense of being an utterly glorious and illustrious display, a "showing forth." In our sacred stories, it is a recognition of the presence of the divine.

In the story of the Epiphany that appears in Matthew's gospel, we hear about the magi, a Greek word used in Jesus' time to identify Babylonian astrologers. They are wise and discerning, persevering and adventurous. It's interesting to note that it is oral tradition and not Scripture that has given them the title of kings, that has chosen their number as three, and has given them names and kingdoms: Balthasar from Arabia, Caspar from India, and Melchior from Persia.

What is significant is that they are gentiles; the first seekers from outside the covenant to find Jesus. They are beckoned by a star, a star that strikes them as remarkable, auspicious, and worthy of investigation. Holding fast to their belief that the star is a sign, a sign of the birth of a King, they set out on what must have been an arduous journey.

They went in faith that the star pointed beyond itself to something miraculous and transforming. And the end of the story tells us that it was exactly that, it was transformational: the kings return another way to their home; they are not the same travelers that had departed.

Just as with the wise ones, epiphanies often happen to us when we are on a journey of some sort and we encounter a moment where something shifts for us. In that moment of suddenly available clarity and fullness, we are able to see God's action in our lives. In those moments when something breaks through our resistance or denial, we are in the experience of epiphany. When we realize that we can't be too young, too smart, too successful, or too cool to be an addict (or to love one), we are having an epiphany. When we listen to a speaker or someone sharing their experience, strength, and hope and we recognize ourselves in their story, we are having an epiphany. Our epiphanies are the bridge between what we understand about grace and a true firsthand experience of God's gracious presence.

Carl Jung, the eminent psychologist, treated Roland, one of AA's early members, whose story is recounted in *Alcoholics Anonymous*. Jung noted, "Here and there, once in a while, alcoholics have had what are called vital spiritual experiences. To me these are phenomena. They appear to be in the nature of huge emotional displacements and rearrangements. Ideas, emotions, and attitudes which were once the guiding forces of the lives of these men are suddenly cast to one side, and a completely new set of conceptions and motives begin to dominate them." The program created an intentional framework for making that journey.

In the program, many of us have experienced what we commonly call "a moment of clarity." In this moment, we have a sense of God's grace breaking in on us. Often, some aspect of the tall and stalwart wall of denial gives way. Something cracks our despair and some morsel of hope appears. Sometimes we notice this gracious reality of God right away. Other times, it is only upon later reflection that we are able to name the grace in a situation. One of the things I have noticed in my own life is that when grace comes to me, it often comes to me through the people with whom I have a relationship. This is my understanding of the term "channel of [God's] peace" in the Prayer of St. Francis. Because of this, I have come to believe in that power greater than ourselves that is everywhere, abundant, full, and inexhaustible, awaiting my recognition and embrace—if I have the grace to see. (TV)

CHRISTMAS—EPIPHANY

The Challenge of Soft Chairs

Soft Chairs or Hard Journey?

■ (CF. MATTHEW 2:1–12)

We thought we could find an easier,
softer way. But we could not.

■ *Alcoholics Anonymous,* PAGE 58

About a dozen years ago, while still a Jesuit priest, I was sitting in an auditorium at Creighton University in Omaha with 400 other men, all Catholic Jesuit priests or brothers. We were gathered for our assembly that took place every two years. This year there was a special buzz in the room as four folks sat in front of us. For the first time in my thirty-five years in that community, we had invited people who worked with us to speak to us about what that experience was like.

One, a dean of students at Marquette in Milwaukee spoke of the privilege of sharing ministry. Another, a French teacher at our high school in Omaha, told how she felt respected as a woman by all these men. Another, a youth minister at a parish we staffed, talked of how interested we all seemed in what he was doing with youth. They were almost three paid endorsements or advertisements. (Understandable, as we paid their salaries.)

Finally, Linda was introduced. Linda was working with us as a volunteer on the Pine Ridge Reservation in Clay County in western South Dakota (which is still, I think, the poorest county in America). Linda mentioned how grateful she was to be among us though, she noted, she was aware that we had never invited any of the Lakota people to speak to us as she was now speaking and we had been among them for more than 100 years.

She was just warming up. She said that she asked the Lakota women in her prayer group what they would say to a group of Jesuit priests if they had the chance to speak to them. The women all hemmed and hawed until the oldest of the group of eight simply said: "Tell them to get back to the people." As Linda reported it to us, the woman then paused a moment, obviously reflecting on what she had just said. She smiled and then said to Linda: "They might not get it so tell it to them this way. Say it like this: Tell them that the softer the chairs, the harder it is to get out of them." Now Linda paused. 401 people sucked all the air out of the room at once. We Jesuits were sitting in that auditorium in pretty cushy chairs. Some of us tried to slide down under them. I have not sat comfortably in a soft chair since.

That is the story that has sat with me all week as I have prayed and reflected on this gospel. Herod and his retinue received the kings, heard the news of the star, were troubled, met secretly with the magi, and sent them on their way, without bothering to join them in their search. They wanted the "easier, softer way" that *Alcoholics Anonymous* speaks of on page 58. No meetings for them, no sponsors for them, no Twelve Steps to the stable for them. They wouldn't get out of their soft chairs and their chosen attitude to join the magi and, as a result, they never experienced the Christ; they never experienced Christmas.

Meanwhile, the magi traveled miles, probably on camels, not exactly in a Mercedes or Lexus, enduring God knows what terrain and weather and eating fast food and sleeping in dingy motels all because they saw a star and it lit up something in them. They were willing to leave all that was familiar and they became willing to live out the consequences as they learned them, because it was so important for them to find the "newborn king of the Jews."

There is a part of us that wants the softer, easier way, much like our drug of choice was for us, except that it was killing us. Then there is the part of us that acknowledges and accepts that life is difficult and that recovery is work.

Life is difficult. That is the first line of Scott Peck's great book *The Road Less Traveled*. Peck acknowledges his debt to the first noble truth of Buddhism: *life is suffering*. As a flaming co-dependent, I so much wanted life to be easy. From my earliest days I was led to think that if I cared for my mother's emotions and fixed her, then all would be well. It didn't really work for me with my mother and it hasn't worked well with any women ever since. But I still would love to think and act out of that belief.

Relationships are difficult. I have to receive you as you are, and I have to show up as I am. I have to respect you and respect me. I have to be honest when I see things differently than you see them. I have to make decisions with you, which means that sometimes I have to submit and sometimes you have to. And that is just the beginning.

Life is difficult. To live my life well, I have to go to bed at a reasonable time, say good night tenderly to my wife, hope and pray for sleep, rise at a reasonable hour, greet my wife, get up and begin my spiritual practice, move from that to the shower and other morning routines, dress for the weather and the activities of the day, proceed with my wife to fix a healthy breakfast, gather what I need for work, and then head out for the rest of my day. When I write it all out like this, I exhaust myself. I could be through for the day by 8:30 am.

Life is difficult. What Scott Peck so brilliantly points out in the beginning of *The Road Less Traveled* is that once we acknowledge and accept that fact, then life just becomes life and we accept it as it is. The wintering chickadee doesn't complain that food and shelter and water are so hard to find in a Minnesota winter. It just sets out each day to live. The wintering maple tree isn't grousing about the lengthy drought and the weather it is experiencing. It just sets out each day to live. Pray God we do the same and honor the magi within us. Life is difficult; relationships are difficult; recovery is difficult. Or, better put: Life is life; relationships are relationships; recovery is recovery. Let's commit to them as they are, and not as we wish they were.

The magi were blessed with a spiritual experience. The promise for us, if we stay faithful to all Twelve Steps, is the same. Can't you just see those three wise ones, Casper, Melchior, and Balthazar, returning to their Twelve-Step group and saying: "Having had a spiritual awakening as the result of our travels, we are trying to carry this message of the Messiah to others, and we are practicing these principles in all our affairs"?

Let us go forth and be the magi, the wise ones, to our brothers and sisters this week. (**DR**)

Flight and "Egypt Time"

When the magi had departed, behold, the angel of the Lord appeared to Joseph in a dream and said, "Rise, take the child and his mother, flee to Egypt, and stay there until I tell you. Herod is going to search for the child to destroy him." ■ MATTHEW 2:13

Then comes the acid test: can we stay sober, keep in emotional balance and live to good purpose under all conditions? A continuous look at our assets and liabilities, and a real desire to learn and grow by this means, are necessities for us. We have learned this the hard way.

■ STEP TEN, *Twelve Steps and Twelve Traditions*

For weeks, we were getting ready for Christmas. We wrapped the presents, laid in the goodies to eat, decorated our homes, put strands of lights on the tree, and gathered with friends and family. And then the big day was here, and, like every other day, it sped past. The wrapping was torn off, the people we gathered headed home, the pine needles scattered on the carpet, and the leftovers were stacked in the refrigerator.

Sometimes, it's a relief to box Christmas back up and get back to business as usual. If we ate too much, traveled too much, or visited too much, we're ready for the return to everyday routine. And if during the holidays we hurt too much, felt alone too much, and remembered too much, the arrival of December 26th is even more welcome.

But the season of Christmas doesn't begin and end in one

day—it goes on for a few weeks. The story of a miraculous birth in the night attended by angels and shepherds is just the beginning. In the season of Christmas we hear other stories, including the story of the angel's visit to Joseph, and his decision to take his wife and their newborn into safety in Egypt.

The story of the flight into Egypt is a perfect reversal of the story of Moses and the exodus of the Jews from their captivity there. Facing a grave threat, Mary and Joseph head beyond the borders of their own land to seek sanctuary, a place where they can protect this tender newborn who has just arrived. Isn't the contrast stark? In one minute, they are welcoming this precious child in peace; in the next they are jarred by the stark reality that he is in grave jeopardy.

This powerful tale, which is full of threats and fear, is also the story of Christmas. It's the part that reminds us that this God of ours did not enter a perfect world, but the real world. The incarnation of Jesus is not only birth into a sort of radically unique divine life but also birth into human life, human life just like ours. And so right away, right after that peaceful story of a starry night in Bethlehem, we see the hostility, danger, and grasping that is the shadow side of human existence, a shadow side that we know very well from our own experience.

Doesn't this align well with our reality? In one minute, we are celebrating with food and gifts, welcoming the Prince of Peace; in the next we're back into the reality of a world bent by poverty, homelessness, illness, war, and death.

Mary and Joseph's story is our story. Just as their lives didn't stand still in Bethlehem, our lives don't stand still either. We also know what it's like to feel fearful and threatened; we particularly know what it's like to feel these feelings within our family units—to worry about a job, to face an illness, to be anxious about college applications, to face deep strain in an important relationship. We know that to be human is to be in the fullness of experience: good and bad; joyful and troubling; peaceful and stressful.

Many people experience a "pink cloud" when they begin recovery. This saying comes from one of the personal stories in *Alcoholics Anonymous*, which refers to a "pink cloud" and "Pink Seven." This is a sort of blissful state that occurs for some folks after they truly surrender to the program, a state in which everything feels just perfect and wonderful. Sadly, like the white clouds in the sky, pink clouds don't seem to last. They dissipate and disappear.

It can be shocking to realize that recovery has not replaced our past with a perfect present but instead has given us an opportunity to come to terms with that past and transform our future. We face the important tasks of taking a personal inventory, admitting wrongs, praying to be relieved of character defects, and making amends to those we have harmed. We have an opportunity to do the important work of growth and change.

We don't know what happened to the Holy Family while they were in Egypt. We know that time passed—Herod died; Jesus grew up. Perhaps Egypt gave Mary and Joseph time to think about the sequence of astonishing events that had so directly touched their lives at his birth. Perhaps Egypt gave them time to embrace what God had done for them.

The Egypt times of our own lives offer us the same thing: time to stop and reflect and ask for God's presence to guide us; time to listen for God's voice in the midst of challenge and turmoil, in the company of our sponsors and with the guidance of the Steps; time to ask, "who are you calling *me* to be, Lord, in this place, in this time?"; time to ask, "who are you calling *us* to be, Lord, this nuclear family, this extended family, this family you gather each week in churches and in meetings around the globe?"

In Egypt time, we learn to "stay sober, keep in emotional balance, and live to good purpose under all conditions." In Egypt time, we stop to nourish and grow the strength of Christ's presence within us as we pray, reflect, and journey with each other. In Egypt time, we deepen our wells of hope and strength, so that hope, peace, joy, and love are in our lives even when we face the power of death and evil—as did Joseph and Mary, and even Jesus Christ himself.

So let's resist saying goodbye to Christmas too quickly. Let's journey together, just as the Holy Family did and as do our communities of recovery. Let's trust and pray that the Christ child who has been born anew will be nourished, protected, and grown in every one of us, particularly in Egypt time. (TV)

Lent

In Lent, the Christian community spends forty days preparing for Easter. In this time, we intentionally turn our hearts and minds to God through practices of prayer, fasting, and alms-giving. At their best, these disciplines are about creating space for spiritual growth and change, not suffering and deprivation.

Lent is a time to embrace our baptismal call with even greater intentionality. In baptism, we become participants in the life, death, and resurrection of Jesus. Our sin is forgiven, and we receive the grace we need to be his active followers. Baptism empowers us to live our faith as Jesus did—with compassion, generosity, courage, and conviction.

No one is a perfect disciple, and Lent is like a spiritual "tune-up." Is our prayer life flat? We can try new prayer forms or make an effort to bring conscious contact with God into existence each day. We can make morning and evening prayer, as well as meditation, a commitment.

Are we dealing with a primary addiction but overlooking other forms of indulgence (Bill and Bob focused on the Seven "Deadly" Sins)? Then we can fast. We can release habits that do not support our recovery, or we can work to remove from our lives habitual ways of relating to people or things that are negative or unhealthy.

Have we become self-centered or too inwardly focused? We can turn outward and give, either monetarily or of our time, to those who would benefit from our "experience, strength and hope."

Lent is a season not of punishment but of mercy. God awaits us with open arms, eager that we return to God. We begin on Ash Wednesday with the beautiful exhortation of the prophet Joel (2:12–13):

> Even now, says the LORD, return to me
>   with your whole heart,
> with fasting, and weeping, and mourning;
> Rend your hearts, not your garments,
>   and return to the LORD, your God.
> (TV)

Facing Temptation

Jesus remained in the desert for forty days, tempted by Satan.

■ **MARK 1:12, 13**

Our next function is to grow in understanding and effectiveness.
This is not an overnight matter. It should continue for our lifetime.
Continue to watch for selfishness, dishonesty, resentment, and fear.
When these crop up, we ask God at once to remove them.

■ *Alcoholics Anonymous*, PAGE 84

Jesus was tempted! He really was human like you and I are! "Temptation" sounds so old-fashioned, so long ago and far away, and yet we recovering folk know that it is right here and right now. Our disease is so cunning and baffling and always here to seduce us. Early on in our recovery we hear the siren voice that sings "Maybe you are not really an addict or alcoholic; maybe you can control your use of that drug." Or we are lulled into remembering how terrific that last high was while tempted to forget how catastrophic it was afterwards. Or we are bullied into thinking that we could never do this sobriety deal for the rest of our lives. And then, when we are "all in" and serious about our recovery, the temptations take on a whole new form. "You are doing so well; let's celebrate your first anniversary of sobriety with a drink." And seven years later we are tempted to think we have mastered this recovery business and can now put it into cruise control. Again and again we succumb to temptation. *Alcoholics Anonymous* tries to remind us to stay daily in our recovery:

> It is easy to let up on the spiritual program of action and rest on our laurels. We are headed for trouble if we do for alcohol is a SUBTLE FOE. We are not cured of alcoholism. What we really have is a daily reprieve contingent on the maintenance of our spiritual condition. (page 85)

Maybe temptations *aren't* so long ago and far away. Maybe W.C. Fields knew too well what he was speaking of when he said, "I can avoid anything except a good temptation."

Jesus was tempted. Since this occurs in all four of the gospels (though in John's gospel it is the crowd that tempts Jesus), it is obviously important to the Spirit of the Scriptures. Also, Christian churches always listen to one or another version of the temptations on the First Sunday of Lent, as a way of framing the season.

In terms of our sacred history, Jesus is being tempted as the New Israel. The Chosen People had their forty years in the desert; Jesus has his forty days.

The Israelites succumbed to temptation three times during those years; Jesus stands up to temptation in his three bouts with it. Two of the Jewish temptations were to complain, once about the manna and once about the quality of the water coming forth from the rock. The other temptation was to be just like their neighbors. Does that sound contemporary? Jesus, on the other hand, never complains and knows he must be his own man.

There are as many interpretations of the temptations as there are economists or meteorologists. These four seem apropos for us in recovery:

First of all, Jesus is being tempted to take his will back,

rather than submit to the will of God. "Use your power egotistically; establish your authority; presume upon your God and take the easier way." To all, Jesus says, "God's will be done, not mine."

A second view of the temptations is that Satan is just slowly chiseling away at Jesus like termites in a building. "Do a good thing whether or not it is for you to do it; let the good end you are about justify the means, even if they are shady at best; take a short cut to your destination." To all Jesus says, "Begone, Satan."

A third view is that Satan attacks Jesus where he is strongest. In wrestling or in debate, our strategy is very different if we size up our opponent as formidable. If weak, we simply overpower him. If strong, we hope to use his strength to carry him right out of the ring. And so Satan attacks Jesus' compassion, his commitment to the Father, and his faith, and hopes Jesus will get cocky and presume upon his strengths. We must know our gifts and, the longer we are in the program, must be continually discerning what really is for us to do, and then do it.

There is a fourth motif that runs through all of the temptations. "I will tell you who you are to be and what you are to do." It is too difficult for any one of us to discern our God-given next step, and so Satan is more than willing to whisper in our ear what that next move is to be. If we give ourselves away to that siren voice, we immediately start sliding down the slippery slope.

You might realize by now that I believe and have experienced that evil is very real and potent, a power other than ourselves. Yes, that is true; though I know the power of God is always stronger if we submit to it. The older and more experienced I am, the more I believe in angels and demons. Evil is personal and tailored differently to each of us. Your temptation might be my grace and vice versa. Each of us must learn to distinguish the Tempter from the Inviter. As Will Rogers said, "Good judgment comes from experience; and most experience comes from bad judgment." We grow wise mainly by learning from our mistakes. So often evil is distorted good and it is always the enemy. It never has our good, our recovery in mind.

So, yes, evil and temptation and Satan are alive and well, but so are God, the Spirit, and angels. It is as though the climax of Paul's Letter to the Ephesians (6:10–18) is written to each of us in recovery:

> Finally, draw your strength from the Lord and from his mighty power. Put on the armor of God so that you may be able to stand firm against the tactics of the devil. For our struggle is not with flesh and blood but with the principalities, with the powers, with the world rulers of this present darkness, with the evil spirits in the heavens. Therefore put on the armor of God, that you may be able to resist on the evil day and, having done everything, to hold your ground. So stand fast with your waist girded in truth, clothed with righteousness as a breastplate, and your feet shod in readiness for the gospel of peace. In all circumstances, hold faith as a shield, to quench all the flaming arrows of the evil one. And take the helmet of salvation and the sword of the Spirit, which is the Word of God. With all prayer and supplication, pray at every opportunity in the Spirit.

That is how I attempt to dress every morning in my prayer and meditation. I hope the same is true for you as well. Blessed Lent and peace on the journey. (DR)

Allowing Ourselves
to Be Loved

"This is my Child, my Son, my Beloved. Listen to Him."
■ **MARK 9:7**

Having had a spiritual awakening...
■ *Alcoholics Anonymous*, **PAGE 60**

God is the Father, and we are His children.
■ *Alcoholics Anonymous*, **PAGE 62**

We call the event in today's gospel "the Transfiguration." It is significant enough to us that we hear one or another version of it every Second Sunday of Lent, and we hear it again when we celebrate the Feast of the Transfiguration on August 6. Obviously, it is a major event for Jesus and for us, his Church, but what does it mean? It is a profoundly mysterious event, one, I would submit, second only to the Resurrection.

If we want to get a taste of the event, let us ask ourselves this question: Have I ever been transformed, deeply changed? What was involved?

Though I have no children of my own, I have been blessed with 15 nephews and nieces and they are all coming of age at once, almost like popcorn.

- In the last year I have watched my niece Sandy being transformed by motherhood as she has become so much softer and gentler with everyone.

- I have watched my niece Melanie being transformed by her pregnancy as she is now so much calmer and more serene.

- I have watched my nephew Mark ask Laurie to marry him and, when she said YES, he suddenly put on his man pants and grew up.

- In my day job as director of spiritual development at a drug and alcohol recovery center, I have watched Erica finally love her life enough to get recovery after multiple relapses and four treatments.

All have been transformed, you could even say transfigured, perhaps not to the extent of Jesus in today's gospel; but all are no longer who they were before. They aren't just different; they haven't just changed; they are significantly different. And all because of love. Nothing transforms us like love—not threats or demands, not money or prestige, not success or failure. Jesus was transformed by Love, by the love of God for him, spoken and acted on just like it was at his baptism. And so it is for us. We all have to come to know God's love from our own experience of hitting bottom. That realization—that God is with us in our lowest, darkest moments—can give us the hope that recovery is possible. No human can do that for us.

Let's look more closely at what is going on in the gospel. Jesus has recently put it to his disciples after they had had some time with him: "Who do you say that I am?" Jesus directly asked them. Peter rose to the occasion and proclaimed,

"You are the Messiah, the Christ." Jesus then began to school the group in the kind of Messiah he was called to be, not a military ruler, but a suffering servant. He urged them to take up their cross of their own lives and follow him. Now, six days later—an important preparation period—Jesus is transfigured into the triumphant Messiah he will be at the end and he is confirmed by the Father's words: "This is my Son, my Beloved."

This is a great connecting event. It connects Jesus back to his baptism and to the God who spoke the same words to him then, to bless and confirm him then as he is doing now. It connects Jesus back to the great Jewish event of the Exodus and to Moses and Elijah, the pillars of Judaism. And it connects him to his future and ours, encouraging him to go on with his mission, telling him that he is on the right path, mysterious as it appears.

God consoles Jesus. *Consolation* is a sacred word in our Christian spirituality. It means I am with you in your solitude. I cannot live your life nor you mine, but I bless you; I encourage you; I reassure you. It is what we are all attempting to give the young hockey player whose spinal cord was severed when he took a hit into the boards. His life has been transfigured and, with his halo, he almost looks like a young man on a cross. And yet aren't we all attempting to console him to go on with his life as it is now and to see what God has in store for him? It is what I was able to offer my friend George recently as he lay dying. I was moved to tell him that all his friends and I loved him too much to ask him to suffer any more and that it was all right for him to die. It is what parents give their children when they remind them that they love them even when a friend refuses to play with them anymore or when they don't make the playoffs or get the part in the play.

Parents especially have the power to make every day a Transfiguration Day in the lives of their children. Every day a parent claims the grace to tell his or her children "I love you" not because of anything they have done or been, but simply because God has blessed us with their presence in our life—that day is a Transfiguration Day. Come to think of it, we all have that power in each other's lives. Maybe, just maybe, the Transfiguration is not so long ago and far away, but could be happening all the time. Maybe, just maybe…. (**DR**)

Quenching Our Thirst

Jesus said to her, "Give me a drink."

■ **JOHN 4:7**

...conscious contact with God...

■ *Alcoholics Anonymous*, **PAGE 59**

Carl Jung gets the credit for coining the phrase "God-thirsty." Supposedly he said that he envied alcoholics because, at their core, they were God-thirsty people. I add: Alcoholics hear the call of God but they respond by going to the wrong address. When they go to the right address, though, the homecoming is *magnificent*.

Jesus comes to the well *thirsty*. The woman comes to the well *thirsty*. She comes to get water, at a safe time for a woman who is an outcast—high noon, in the heat of the day, when no other self-respecting woman would be there. He comes, obviously physically thirsty—he is human after all—but also thirsty for her, not in a sexual or physical way, but for her soul.

He is the one who asks for a drink—he breaks all the boundaries, those between men and women, between Jews and Samaritans—and she responds and engages him. What follows is the longest conversation in the New Testament. Jesus is speaking like a well-digger, always inviting the woman deeper. She tries to distract the conversation, but then hangs in and goes deeper with Jesus.

There is a passage in the *Catechism* that summarizes the conversation succinctly and accurately: "Christ comes [to the well] to meet every human being. It is he who first seeks us and asks us for a drink. Jesus thirsts; his asking arises from the depths of God's desire for us. Whether we realize it or not, prayer is the encounter of God's thirst with ours. God thirsts that we may thirst for [God]" (*Catechism of the Catholic Church*, no. 2560).

You and I are thirsty. We thirst for *union*—to *be one*. We thirst for *home*—to *belong*. We thirst for *fullness*—to *fill our awful emptiness*. However you put the object of our deepest thirst, we are a thirsty people.

And we have tried almost everything else by the time we have come to God—alcohol, heroin, vicodin, cocaine, oxy-contin, gambling, sex, food, co-dependent relationships— have I missed anything? They all promised everything but they ended up delivering nothing.

Jesus promises one thing—in the Twelve Steps, we call it "conscious contact"—and for us that is everything, as day by day, little by little, by doing our prayer and meditation, we realize we are in *union*, we are *at home*, we are *full* today, the only day we have. We will need to come back to the well again tomorrow, but as for today, our thirst is satisfied.

Thank God for our sobriety, our recovery, our being awake today! (DR)

Coming to Faith

"He put clay on my eyes, and I washed, and now I can see."

■ JOHN 9:15

Having had a spiritual awakening as THE* *result of these steps,...*

■ *Alcoholics Anonymous,* PAGE 60

*[in *Alcoholics Anonymous* it's *a* result]

Recently in Lent we heard the gospel of Jesus and the woman at the well and we commented on how she is all of us, "God-thirsty," as we are, in Carl Jung's term. Now we hear the gospel of Jesus and the man born blind, the one who is "God-sighted," as the leaders are "God-blind."

Let me explain what I mean in recovery terms, yours and mine. A few years ago I was at a concert of sacred music and, after a particularly moving piece, one of the musicians shouted out, "The opposite of faith is not doubt, but certainty." That so struck me then and now. We live in a culture so addicted to certainty or, to use a synonym, to clarity. It is simply another form of control or trying to get power over someone or something. We even say "I see what you mean," when we aren't seeing anything but have convinced ourselves that now we know for sure. So are the religious leaders in today's Gospel—they have convinced themselves that Jesus is not the Messiah because he does not keep the Sabbath as they keep the Sabbath.

They are so certain that he is not the Messiah that they cannot see that he has healed the man born blind.

God will never give us so much certainty or so much clarity that we no longer need God. We are powerless over our Higher Power. Read that again. We are so addicted to power and control that we are disappointed and walk away when God does not act as we think God should act or, more crassly, when God does not answer our prayers as we want them answered. Instead, we are given faith, belief in a caring Higher Power who day by day is faithful, giving us everything we need, if not everything we want.

It is also important for us to realize that the man born blind comes slowly to faith in Jesus as we come slowly into the fullness of recovery. At first he calls him "the man they call Jesus." Then, in debate with the Pharisees, he is inspired to call Jesus a "prophet." Later, Jesus asks him if he believes in Jesus as "the Son of Man." The man bows down and worships Jesus as his Lord, Lord of heaven and earth. That is the fullness of faith. So too we typically come slowly into recovery and wherever we are is just fine. At first we are content to be sober, and then slowly we regain our physical and emotional health and our relational and social health. Now we are in recovery. And yet what still awaits us, as we climb all twelve of the steps, is a full spiritual awakening. We wake up, just as the man finally saw Jesus as Lord, to the caring God of the Third Step who is with us every moment of every day. In the daylight of that realization we see ourselves as beloved by God, undeserving and unworthy as we are. This God of ours loves us, not because *we* are worthy but because *God* is worthy. And we see one another and all creation as beautiful and beloved by God. And we find we want to genuflect and reverence everyone and everything.

We, who have been so blind to the presence and activity of God and to our own beauty and goodness and that of one another, are beginning to see. Thank God we are beginning to see! (**DR**)

Living with Paradox

"Unless the grain of wheat falls to the earth and dies, it remains just a grain of wheat. But if it dies, it produces much fruit." ■ JOHN 12:24

We never apologize to anyone for depending upon our Creator. We can laugh at those who think spirituality the way of weakness. Paradoxically, it is the way of strength.

■ *Alcoholics Anonymous,* PAGE 68

PARADOXICALLY—now *there* is a 50-cent word! (It does *not* mean two doctors in partnership.) It means something that is contrary to logic—to our heads—but true to our experience, if we will get out of our heads where we are the kings and queens of control and simply reflect on the truth of our experience.

One of the most obvious paradoxes is "the only way to get more love is to give it away." That doesn't make sense to our heads—we don't get more of anything by giving it away. But it is true of love. If we try to control our love or try to control the beloved, we end up destroying the love, the beloved, and the relationship. If we only concern ourselves with loving, we get more love both in the giving and the receiving.

The same is true of today's gospel, the most significant image, the most profound paradox in Christianity. Today we are celebrating the Fifth Sunday of Lent. Next Sunday is Palm Sunday, which begins Holy Week—the great week of paradoxes for Christians. Jesus must die to rise. Easter Sunday can only come after Good Friday. Today, in this twelfth chapter of John's gospel, Jesus is already anticipating Holy Week. The grain must die to produce life. The container of hyacinths is producing flowers only because the bulbs have broken open—died—that life might come forth. It doesn't make sense to our intellects. But if we had just held these bulbs in our hands and said, "Prove that planting these will produce flowers," we would be holding dying bulbs all our lives. At some point, as *Alcoholics Anonymous* goes on to say on page 68, we need to claim the courage to trust God and then place the bulbs in the ground. With time and sun and air and water—and with the care of God—we watch the flowers emerging.

I submit to you that at some point in our lives, if our recovery is real and profound and if our following of Jesus is faithful, our lives become profoundly paradoxical. There is a point in Luke's gospel where Jesus turns and says to us, after we have been following him for a while, "Whoever wishes to save his life will lose it; but whoever loses his life for my sake will save it" (Luke 9:24). From that point on, in Luke's gospel as in John's, all of life becomes paradoxical. I suggest that the same is true for one working the Steps. As page 68 indicates, when one moves from fear to courage and really entrusts one's life to God, one commences to outgrow fear and all of life becomes paradoxical, and we begin to realize the truth of statements like these, all words of Jesus:

» "If you exalt yourself, you shall be humbled. If you humble yourself, you shall be exalted." *(Matthew 23:12)*

» "Anyone among you who aspires to greatness must serve the rest, and whoever wants to rank first must serve the needs of all." *(Matthew 20:27)*

» "Go, sell what you have, and give to the poor and you
will have treasure in heaven; then come, follow me."
(Mark 10:21)

Think of it: Are not our recoveries based on paradox? Is it not
true that we have had to get out of our heads and our con-
trolling minds to acknowledge the truth of our experience?

• Haven't we had to acknowledge our powerlessness over
drugs and alcohol to gain any power in our own lives?

• Haven't we had to surrender our wills because our willfulness kept driving us back to relapse or co-dependency?

• Haven't we had to acknowledge the exact nature of our
wrongs to experience forgiveness and to finally let go of
our shame and guilt?

• Haven't we had to embrace paradox to begin and continue our recovery?

In my life a caring God has brought me through the Good
Friday of Alcoholism to the Easter Sunday of Recovery. That
same caring God has brought me through death to a fuller,
richer life than I could have ever imagined. I submit the same
has been true for you, *is* true for you, and, most importantly,
will be true for you.

Thanks be to God. **(DR)**

Trusting the Power of Inventory

"Do not think that I have come to abolish the law or the prophets. I have come not to abolish but to fulfill. Amen, I say to you, until heaven and earth pass away, not the smallest letter or the smallest part of a letter will pass from the law." ■ MATTHEW 5:17–18

This thought brings us to Step Ten, which suggests we continue to take personal inventory and continue to set right any new mistakes as we go along. We vigorously commenced this way of living as we cleaned up the past. We have entered the world of the Spirit. Our next function is to grow in understanding and effectiveness. This is not an overnight matter. It should continue for our lifetime. Continue to watch for selfishness, dishonesty, resentment, and fear. When these crop up, we ask God at once to remove them. We discuss them with someone immediately and make amends quickly if we have harmed anyone. Then we resolutely turn our thoughts to someone we can help. Love and tolerance of others is our code. ■ *Alcoholics Anonymous*, PAGE 84

There's nothing quite like singing in the church choir to help me focus on the themes of any given liturgical season, because when you're in the choir and you sing every song four or five times as you rehearse, things get crystal clear! This is particularly true in Lent when in song we hear God's voice: "I have promised my covenant to all who will hear…." "Come back to me, with all your heart...." The hymns of Lent are, really without exception, very beautiful songs of God's promise and fidelity.

In the Sermon on the Mount, Jesus makes it clear that the promises made by God to Israel remain true, and that Jesus' followers are children of the Covenant and bound by the law. Jesus is quite explicit: He reminds us that he is not with us to set aside the law. Instead, he tells us that through him the law is *fulfilled*—not a "jot or a tittle," the smallest strokes in the Hebrew alphabet, changes with his arrival.

When Jesus speaks of the law, he is referencing the five books of the Torah. In these five books, we find two huge themes. First, we find the rule book. We are given the commandments that define who we are as a people. Jews and Christians alike recognize the commandments as the core of our relationship with God. Whenever we are not living true to the commandments, Catholics are encouraged to reconcile ourselves to God and one another in the sacrament of reconciliation.

The Tenth Step serves us in the same spirit. When we are wrong, we are to promptly admit it and restore right relationship with other people. It is in Step Ten that we hear that there is actually a right use of human will: every day is a day when we must carry the vision of God's will into all of our activities. "How can I best serve Thee—Thy will (not mine) be done. These are thoughts that must go with us constantly. We can exercise our will power along this line all we wish. It is the proper use of the will."

Once, while leading an eighth-grade faith group, I had an experience that really expanded my understanding of the place of both the commandments and ongoing reflection in my life. I was preparing to share with the youth the principle that we are called to reconciliation when we are in a state of grave sin—when we have broken one of the commandments. And I was really minimizing this in my mind: I was pretty confident that none of them had killed anyone recently or coveted their neighbor's middle-aged wife. (I was pretty sure, however, that most of them had not honored their mother and father, if my house was representative!) And then I came across a very powerful inventory for teens.

It asked questions like these: Do you worship the false gods of status, consumerism, or peer approval? Do you use language you'd never use in front of your grandmother? Do you use people for your selfish pleasure? Do you envy or resent the popularity or success of others?

As I worked through this inventory, I began to see, in very powerful ways, how I am called, personally, to live both the letter of these commandments and their spirit. I am called to live under the law and to tune myself to God's love and will. Our searching and fearless moral inventory of the Fourth Step begins the process of building a muscle we will need to look honestly at each day in our Tenth Step.

This takes me to the second aspect of Jesus' affirmation of the Torah. In the Torah, in addition to receiving the law, we have laid out for us the astonishing, miraculous story of the covenant, first with Noah, then Abraham and Sarah, then Moses. The Torah is not just about rules. The Torah is also about the promise God has made to every one of us that God will be with us, faithfully, unendingly. The God of Torah, the God of Jesus, is the God of love, the God of forgiveness, the God who will not, can not, be separated from each of us, no matter how we stumble, no matter how we fail.

In light of God's love for us, in light of God's fidelity, the law becomes freedom, not a burden. The law becomes not the thing that oppresses us, but the thing that frees us to deepen our connection to one another, to God. The law becomes a loving guide by which we can make an honest assessment of where we are and, as the song I mentioned earlier states, return to God, the source of grace and mercy, with all our heart. When we first encounter the Steps, we may feel overwhelmed and fearful. It is only by staying close to other people in the program and hearing about their journeys that we come to see that the work that intimidates us is actually the pathway to freedom.

The British author G.K. Chesterton said that the problem with Christianity is not that it's been tried and been found wanting, it's that it has been found difficult and left not tried at all. But I say that the difficulty of living under the law falls away when we see that we do not live this life alone; we live it in the company of a faithful community, in a circle of love and acceptance in the rooms, and in the company of a God of abiding love. (TV)

Focusing on Today

"Thy kingdom come..."

■ MATTHEW 6:10

Clear away the wreckage of your past. Give freely of what you find and join us. We shall be with you in the Fellowship of the Spirit, and you will surely meet some of us as you trudge the Road of Happy Destiny. May God bless you and keep you—until then.

■ *Alcoholics Anonymous*, PAGE 164

At the close of countless Twelve-Step meetings, these three familiar words, "Thy Kingdom come," are spoken. They are part of the best-known prayer in the Christian world, the Lord's Prayer. But what exactly do we mean when we pray them? What is it that we want to come? And what is our role in having this kingdom, this reign of God, appear among us?

The idea of God's kingdom was not new to Jesus' listeners. Jesus did not invent the phrase; it appears in multiple places in the psalms, and the books of Isaiah, Daniel, and Zechariah. The *Kaddish*, as it was prayed long before Jesus was born, said: "May He let His Kingdom rule...speedily and soon."

Jews who lived at the time of Jesus had a particular understanding of the "kingdom of God." It was not metaphorical. It was literally a kingdom. They eagerly wanted God to send them a leader who would throw off Roman rule and make Judea an independent nation again—a nation of righteousness, glory, and blessings. The Dead Sea Scrolls and other writings of the time show that the Jews wanted and expected the messiah to be a kingly leader. Some even expected two Messiahs—a kingly one and a priestly one.

Into this climate—filled with eager but vague expectations of God's intervention—John the Baptist and Jesus preached the nearness of God's kingdom. But the kingdom Jesus spoke of proved to be *nothing* like the popular expectation.

Unlike others of his time, Jesus did not announce a kingdom that was far off in the future. Rather, he spoke of something that is being built at this very minute, something that started with Creation but was happening right in that very moment:

» The kingdom of God is at hand. *(Matthew 4:17)*

» The kingdom of God is in the midst of you. *(Luke 17:21)*

» The kingdom of God has come upon you. *(Matthew 12:28)*

For Jesus, the kingdom of God is about this moment and this place, in which the Higher Power is present and real. The kingdom of Jesus is not a new imperial rule but a new sort of relationship with each other and with God.

For Jesus, the kingdom of heaven is a kingdom that comes *from* heaven to this very moment, as well as a kingdom that exists *in* heaven. It is not just a future state of bliss at the end of human history (or at the end of our individual lives), but a possibility right now, something that is already here.

There is a Jewish folktale about a poor man named Isaac who lived in Krakow. He began having a vivid dream in which he saw a box holding a treasure. It was hidden under a bridge in a city far from his home. After dreaming of this many times, Isaac decided that he must make the long trip to investigate. He walked more than 300 miles. To his delight and astonishment, he found the bridge but before he could dig for the treasure, the police came and arrested him. They were suspicious: What was Isaac, a Jew, doing under the bridge in this gentile section of the city?

He told them about his dream, but they only laughed at him. Mocking him, one of the officers said that he, too, had been dreaming of a treasure, but it was buried under the stove of a peasant named Isaac who lived in Krakow! But the powerful officer was not going to waste his time and money following a stupid dream. Finally, the officers were done mocking Isaac, and they released him, telling him to go home and forget this foolishness. Filled with energy, Isaac rushed home, making the longer journey in even less time. Running to his stove, he began to dig, and there he found a buried treasure so vast that he lived with great wealth, secure for the rest of his days.

Sometimes, keeping the focus on today can be revelatory. As Isaac discovered, there may be treasures before us that we would miss if our gaze were regretfully focused on the past or anxiously cast upon the future.

Focusing *on this moment in this day* is a spiritual exercise we receive through the program. Its spirit is expressed in many of our slogans, "One Day at a Time," "First Things First," "Just for Today," "Live Life on Life's Terms." One of the reflections in the Al-Anon book *Courage to Change* puts it beautifully: "I am writing my life story with every single *today*." (TV)

GOOD FRIDAY

Facing the Cross

*Jesus said to Peter, "Put your sword into its scabbard.
Shall I not drink the cup that the Father gave me?"*

■ JOHN 18:11

*Whenever we fail any of these people, we can promptly admit it—
to ourselves always, and to them also, when the admission would
be helpful. Courtesy, kindness, justice, and love are the keynotes by
which we may come into harmony with practically anybody. When in
doubt we can always pause, saying, "Not my will, but Thine, be done."
And we can often ask ourselves, "Am I doing to others as I would
have them do to me—today?"*

■ STEP TEN, *Twelve Steps and Twelve Traditions*, PAGE 93

I remember Good Friday 2002. The very prayer that evening
asked us to pause and remember another day, a Tuesday the
previous September. For many of us, that day really did feel
like a crucifixion. Certainly that was the case for my family
when we realized that my cousin, John Gallagher, was dead
in the World Trade Center's rubble. I'm sure there were other people in the assembly who shared that particular day
of crucifixion with us—perhaps you do, as well. But maybe
your day wasn't September 11. Maybe your day was in July
or February or December. Maybe your day wasn't in 2001.
Maybe it was in 1980 or 1963 or 1944.

Human life can be so wonderful, but it also can be so devastating. Why is it that at some point or another, all of us seem to stand, like Jesus, face to face with the cross?

Good Friday is the day in which ritual brings the cross to the front and center of our consciousness once again. It's interesting to note that the cross is not the oldest symbol of the Christian story. In the first centuries after the death of Jesus, Christians did not observe Good Friday. For them, the cross was a symbol of a ghastly form of public torture. It was not something they found comforting—they preferred to focus on the risen Christ, not the human, suffering Jesus on the cross.

John's gospel, written near the end of the first century, shares this avoidance of the issue of Jesus' human suffering. The other gospel accounts of the passion have a very human quality to them—we see Jesus' fear and hesitation, he tells us of his abandonment. John does not focus on any of those themes. For John, the divinity of Jesus is always at the forefront. This is the gospel that begins "In the beginning was the word...." The crucifixion is the completion of forces set in motion at the dawn of time.

Why is John's depiction of Jesus so different from that of the other writers? Among other things, he is writing for people who are alienated and displaced—people who have been expelled from worship in the synagogue. They're in conflict with the greater Jewish community and they're mad. They want to place blame on those who are excluding them.

It's important for us to place John's gospel in its historical context because this particular depiction of the trial and death of Jesus, which includes global references to the Jews, was used to persecute the Jewish people for millennia. Theologians who have studied these events believe that, in fact, it was only a small faction of Temple authorities, fearing that Jesus was a threat, that brought him into the justice system of their oppressors. It is likely that Jesus was executed by Rome without so much as a second thought, despite the depiction of Pilate that John offers.

There is a saying that's helpful when one grapples with sacred stories like this one, and it goes like this: "All stories are true, and some of them really happened." So even if we know that not all of the events happened just as we heard John depict them, we still ask what this story has to say to us that is still very true.

I think it imparts many truths, but the one that really jumps out at me is that this sacred story reminds us that our God is God is in the flesh. Jesus has experienced everything that life entails—he's walked, breathed, eaten, slept, and celebrated with his friends. *The Constitution on the Church in the Modern World* of Vatican II says it really well: "He worked with human hands; he thought with a human mind. He acted with a human will, and with a human heart he loved." We also know that he experienced firsthand the forces that wound us: loss, grief, betrayal, victimization, suffering, and death. He was fully God we believe, but he also was fully human.

Just think about that. This is a very unique God, this God of ours. Jesus does not stand outside creation wielding amazing cosmic powers. He's right in it with all of us. When we really let that in, when we let in the Incarnation, we begin to touch the astonishing reality of what Jesus meant then, and what Jesus means for all time.

The Incarnation is not something frozen in time 2000 years ago, but something that lives in each of us. There are no first-century Jewish rabbis from Galilee in our lives today. But we can still feel him here among us, dwelling in our midst. The incarnation means the risen Christ in you and me.

When we touch this, our relationship to the world is transformed:

- We see hungry children, here and abroad, and we see the Body of Christ.

- We see those suffering from a global AIDS pandemic and we see the Body of Christ.

- We see the grief of those mourning a murdered child, and we see the Body of Christ.

- We see the still sick and suffering addict, and we see the Body of Christ.

In Jesus the Christ, we believe ourselves, our world, our suffering, and our death are transformed. When we encounter the great heartbreaks and challenges of life, we can face them with resolve and faith, and like Jesus—and, as suggested in our program—say "Not my will, but thine be done." (TV)

Easter

Easter is typically a big day for Christians. There are hosts of ways that people celebrate and countless cultural expressions. My earliest memories of Easter are the lovely new dresses my grandmother would buy for my sisters and me at Cornell's department store in the Bronx. In addition to a lovely dress, there would be fancy socks, gloves, and a hat. Yes, I am that old.

Today, my Easter focus is less on attire and more on hospitality. There is the annual debate between the lamb and the ham factions of my family. My sister brings a gorgeous cake in the shape of an Easter egg, with spectacular piping. I indulge my inner Martha Stewart in different ways every year, varying my tablecloths and other appointments. Yes, I am that corny.

But the day after Easter, after the clothes are in the hamper and the feast consumed, we have always quickly moved on to the next thing. It was many years before I registered that Easter is not just a day, but an entire season. It turns out that resurrection is something to be held close, celebrated, and rejoiced over for weeks, not a single day.

I think recovering people have a particular understanding of the miracle of Easter and why we might not want to let it go so quickly. Most people get into the meeting rooms after some experience of suffering and death in their lives tied to their own addiction or the addiction of someone they love. People who have embraced the program and seen their lives transformed understand in a real way that the God we believe in is the God of liberation, who has truly conquered sin and death. (TV)

"Practicing Resurrection"

We are Resurrection People: Easter is our Feast.

■ JOHN 20:11-18

"Go to my brothers and tell them,
'I am going to my Father and your Father, to my God and your God.'"
Mary went and announced to the disciples,
"I have seen the Lord."

■ JOHN 20:17-18

If we are painstaking about this phase of our development, we will
be amazed before we are half way through. We are going to know a
new freedom and a new happiness. We will not regret the past nor
wish to shut the door on it. We will comprehend the word serenity
and we will know peace. No matter how far down the scale we have
gone, we will see how our experience can benefit others. That feeling of
uselessness and self-pity will disappear. We will lose interest in selfish
things and gain interest in our fellows. Self-seeking will slip away. Our
whole attitude and outlook upon life will change. Fear of people and
of economic insecurity will leave us. We will intuitively know how to
handle situations which used to baffle us. We will suddenly realize
that God is doing for us what we could not do for ourselves.

■ *Alcoholics Anonymous,* PP. 83–84

There are four accounts of the resurrection in the gospels, and each features loyal, brave, and loving Mary of Magdala, who goes to the tomb of Jesus after three days have passed to anoint his body. Today, we call her the Apostle to the Apostles, the first person to proclaim that Christ is risen. We might say that Mary of Magdala is truly the first Easter person.

You have to love Mary's tenacity and loyalty. Everything the community hoped for is in wrack and ruin. But despite her grief, she musters the energy to take the next right step. She's going to do the rituals. She doesn't seem concerned that she may be threatened or obstructed. She will be a good Jew and attend to the body of her beloved "Rabbouni." And she heads out, despite considerable anguish and copious tears.

Because we have heard the resurrection narratives so often, we can lose track of the fact that every one of them begins with deep desperation and terrible loss. All that the disciples and followers hoped for, all of their joy at impending liberation, have been crushed under the boot heel of Rome. They are in chaos and fear. They are plunged into darkness and death. Some have given up and left Jerusalem. Others are hiding in fear. Mary stands before the tomb, desperately weeping.

Being cast into the depths of despair is an experience most of us will have at some point in our lives. Very few of us get to avoid it. My first experience came when I was thirteen, when my father died suddenly and unexpectedly at the age of forty. I remember climbing into bed that night in total pain—emotional pain so extreme that my body literally hurt. As I closed my eyes, a sense of relief came over me when I thought, "It will be over soon, because I will die tonight." I really believed that no one could stay alive feeling the way I was feeling. Surely, my life would end as I slept and my agony would be over.

Imagine my disappointment and surprise when I woke up. What I didn't realize at that young age, but what I have come to understand as I have grown older and have experienced other seasons of grief, is that the human spirit is incredibly resilient. We wake back up from the darkness of sleep. We keep breathing. We keep walking. The days pass. Eventually, our hearts, minds, and bodies don't hurt quite so much. Our suffering softens. I still miss my father decades later, but now I think of him with peace, not heartache. I discovered that I am very resilient.

As I have come to deeper understanding of my faith, and as I have watched, over and over again, the miracle of recovery, I have come to believe—and believe deeply—that human beings are not merely resilient: they are, in fact, made for resurrection. For the most part, we don't just endure, we transform and transcend. That is what the Christ demonstrated to us in his paschal journey. We may suffer and die, but, like our Rabbouni, we can rise again.

Perhaps the biggest challenge we face every time life brings us suffering or death is to trust this pattern Christ revealed to us. I've been watching my teen daughter go crazy with a Rubik's cube, a toy that became popular when I was her age. She sits for hours, turning and trying new configurations, muttering and generally going a little crazy. But she sticks to it. Why? She actually got it a few times! She knows the pattern will work out, but she doesn't know how many turns or how much patience it will take to get there.

Having faith that we will move through our greatest difficulties requires a similar hope and endurance. We must choose to believe we will get there, that we, like others, can transcend.

"Keep coming," we say to the newcomer. "It will work if you work it." Trust us.

My coauthor and friend Dick put it this way: "Jesus spends a lot of Easter Sunday telling the disciples that things had to be exactly the way they are. That is true in the life of each of us and the communities in which we find ourselves. Everything has been exactly as it was meant to be. Our entire history is sacred. None of it is to be wished away. We are who we are today because of all the comings and goings, struggles and reconciliations, departures and joinings, givings and takings that have been ours. Because of that, we want to tell the story just like Mary Magdalene and those disciples running back from Emmaus. Something very good is happening here for our faith and our recovery."

This is the hope we hold out in the rooms. I was meeting recently with a woman I sponsor, also a minister, and we were deeply grieving something that had just happened in our country. We were scared, angry, hurt, and shaky. Sitting with our coffee and bagels, we soon moved past our angst and fear and began talking about the journey of recovery. We reminded each other that, one day at a time, our most devastating train wrecks have become life's miraculous starting points. That from the ashes, we have seen people rise, Phoenix-like, to new life. We remembered that "God has wrought miracles among us," as *Alcoholics Anonymous* says. We took some time out to remember and, despite everything, to be grateful. In both our experiences, love triumphed. We believe it will again. Like our sister Mary, we are resurrection people.

There is a beautiful poem by Wendell Berry that has great meaning for me, particularly the last line: "Practice resurrection." That's what my friend and I were doing. That's what we do in our parish communities. That's what we help people do in our Twelve-Step rooms. Because we know that we had been weeping, but that then we had "seen the Lord." (TV)

Awakening Spiritually

"Unless I see the mark of the nails in his hands,... I will not believe."

■ JOHN 20:25

Having had a spiritual awakening...

■ *Alcoholics Anonymous*, PAGE 60

The Sundays between Easter and Pentecost are celebrated as the Sundays *of* Easter, not *after* Easter. This is an important distinction. We are praying to remain in the Spirit of Jesus risen. As resurrected people ourselves, that should not be difficult. We rejoice in Jesus risen! We rejoice in our rising, our awakening.

The gospel of the Second Sunday of Easter features Thomas, the twin. He just might be the twin of all of us in recovery. We call him the Doubter, but today he becomes the great Believer.

About fifteen years ago there was a TV series called *Nothing Sacred*. It was a popular evening show, but it ran for only about eight months. It was about a liberal Catholic parish, and it ended because of the numerous complaints of conservative Catholics that it was too liberal for their tastes. I had the chance to see the last show produced but never shown on television.

In that show, the church had suffered a fire on Easter night. Now it was the next Sunday, the Second Sunday of Easter.

The question was who was going to preside and preach at the Sunday service. The pastor was unavailable because he was injured in fighting the fire as it was flaring up. The associate was unavailable because he was too embarrassed to show his face—the fire began after he locked up the church after the last service on Easter, and he had not noticed that candles were left burning. Eventually they set fire to the altar cloths. No one else on the staff could preside or preach. Finally, Father John, the old retired priest who resided in the rectory, raised his hand and said that he would preach. Everyone was surprised because he had not presided or preached for at least four years. Imagine how curious everyone was when he rose to preach. He began: "It has been four years to the day since I preached from this pulpit. The reason for that is that only on that Sunday did I realize that Jesus still had his wounds after the resurrection. I did not want a God who still had his wounds on the other side of his victory. Then we had our fire and the struggle we each have had with it since and I realized that Thomas needed Jesus to still have his wounds because they provided Thomas with access to Jesus. 'I will believe only if I see his wounds.' How else could Thomas have made his way back into Jesus' good graces? And Jesus showed him his wounds. We need Jesus to have his wounds because we have our wounds and the wounds of Jesus match up with ours and compassionately touch ours. 'By his wounds our wounds are healed.' And so I stand and preach again and give thanks for his wounds and for ours."

Jesus stands before us as the defeated victorious one and as the wounded healer. We stand before him as the defeated recovering ones and as wounded healers ourselves. We are having a spiritual awakening.

We could speak as to what a "spiritual awakening" is and how one occurs but today I would rather address what is it we awaken *to* when we wake up. I propose we wake up to three realities:

1. *Our God, our higher power, truly is a Caring God.* The Third Step is right: our God cares for us. God does not fix us, make it all better, or completely cure us. God hangs in with us, gives us what we need to take the next right step and do the next right thing. God aches with us, grieves with us at what we have experienced, is even angry with us at how we have suffered. And then God gives us what we need to keep walking the recovery path.

2. *We are the beloved of God.* We haven't received everything we might have wanted, but we have gotten what we needed to remember that all comes from God and all returns to God. We are not here because we are victims or to feel sorry for one another. We are here so we can encourage each other in gratitude and in response to our God.

3. *We wake up to the fact that at some cellular level and in the mind of God we are all one.* That was the final prayer of Jesus in John's gospel before he went to his passion. "May they all be one, as you, Father, are in me and I in you. May they all be one in us" (John 17:21). Here is how Albert Einstein, maybe the greatest mind of our lifetime, put it: "A human being is part of the whole called by us the universe....Our task must be to free ourselves from this prison (of our delusion that we are separate) by widening our circle of love and compassion to embrace all living creatures and the whole of nature in its beauty."

Thank you, Albert Einstein. And thank you, Jesus Christ.
(DR)

Following the Good Shepherd

"I am the good Shepherd."

■ **JOHN 10:11**

Therefore, no society of men and women ever had a more urgent NEED
*for continuous effectiveness and permanent unity. We alcoholics see
that we must work together and hang together, else most of us will
finally die alone.* ■ *Alcoholics Anonymous*, PAGE 164

As we continue to celebrate the Easter season, lingering in
the joy and promise of resurrection, we are hopefully awakening more and more to the appearances of our risen God
in our midst today and enjoying our waking up and our recovery. Within that frame, every fourth Sunday of Easter we
hear some section of the tenth chapter of John's gospel, the
chapter that treats of Jesus as the Good Shepherd.

Early on in my seminary years I realized that I would be
preaching on a number of Scriptures that had to do with
sheep and shepherds and, as a city boy, I was not sure of the
difference between a calf and a sheep. So I sought out opportunities to interview shepherds and to observe sheep. I
have been blessed to have those opportunities from Milbank,
South Dakota, to the Holy Land, from Guatemala to India.
Early on, walking in pastures of sheep, I observed that sheep

are skittish and refuse to learn from each other. They insist on bouncing into fences just like the one ahead of them did. They eat the grass down to the roots and also have a gland that secretes an ointment that has an odor other animals detest. Yet every part of a sheep from wool to hooves is valuable for something to humans. Also, sheep flock together. They are more like us than we might like to think.

Shepherds revealed to me that they intimately know each of their sheep and would die for them. The best example of that came when I was in the highlands of Guatemala and had the chance to visit Pedro, a shepherd who had recently lost his wife in childbirth. I was visiting a friend, Sr. Mary Bertand, who was attending to Pedro and his family in their grief, and we decided to stop and see Pedro. As we walked his land with him, I asked him through Sr. Mary's translating for both of us, how many sheep he had. He turned away and only later did I realize that he was unschooled and could not count. In his embarrassment he said nothing. Fortunately, I blundered into the silence and asked him how he would know if he lost one. He straightened up and proudly proclaimed, "If I lost one, I would know it right away." How much like Jesus Pedro is. Jesus knows and loves each one of us and lives and dies and rises for each one of us.

In our lives of recovery what are examples of shepherding and being shepherded? I submit that it is *sponsoring* and *being sponsored*.

You and I know that the words *sponsor* and *sponsoring* are not in *Alcoholics Anonymous*, the "Big Book" of AA. The phenomenon of sponsoring seems to have started in the hospital in Akron at which Dr. Bob and Sr. Ignatia were staff members. The hospital insisted that, if people were going to be admitted for detoxing and early treatment, they had to have a sponsor who would be financially responsible for any bills and also available to meet with the alcoholic and the alcoholic's family as recovery occurred.

By 1944 sponsorship had so developed that the Cleveland AA community published a pamphlet on the subject, emphasizing that sponsorship is for the benefit of the sponsee—and, indirectly, for the sponsor—but it is not an ego-massaging accomplishment of the sponsor. The sponsor is to share her story with the new sponsee, to instill confidence in the sponsee, to encourage reading of *Alcoholics Anonymous*, to talk of spirituality and of faith if the occasion presents itself, and to be available to the sponsee's family—all ingredients of good sponsorship to this day.

That is remarkable shepherding, and so important to our recovery. I submit that you learn much of the quality of one's recovery by the quality of one's relationship to a sponsor. I say that particularly because my sponsor recently died and I wanted to properly grieve George before I sought another sponsor. But the time has come, and I have found someone new to accompany me on my recovery journey.

Please let these words encourage you as well, especially if you have no sponsor at this time. Why pass up a graced opportunity for accountability and encouragement? Why pass up the chance to offer a brother or a sister the opportunity to be of service to us? We did say that we would go to any lengths, didn't we? **(DR)**

Connecting to the Higher Power

"I am the vine; you are the branches."

■ JOHN 15:5

*"My Creator, I am now willing that you
should have all of me...."*

■ *Alcoholics Anonymous*, PAGE 76

As we continue to celebrate the Easter season and our spiritual awakening, we reflect on who this *higher power* really is; for us Christians, who this Jesus truly is. On the Fourth Sunday of Easter, the topic is "I am the Good Shepherd; you are my sheep." On the Sixth Sunday, it will be "Greater love than this has no one." On the Fifth Sunday of Easter, it is "I am the Vine; you are the branches."

The vine was a favorite image for Jesus' original Jewish listeners. A rabbi once explained to me that the vine was the first domesticated plant for the Jewish people as they settled in Israel. It quickly became an image in Scripture for the Jewish community itself (Isaiah 5). It is a plant very dependent on the skill of the vine-dresser and on the rhythm of the seasons. It is also remarkably versatile as it can creep, climb, or do whatever its environment demands. At the same time the vine is worth nothing except for its fruit—the grape.

In this gospel passage, Jesus applies this image to himself. "I am the Vine; you are the branches." In a backdoor sort of way he answers the question: What is it to be fruitful, to be productive, to make a significant difference? This question becomes very important to us in our 40s and 50s and as we climb the Twelfth Step. Erik Erikson, the developmental psychologist, once said that if we are not concerned in nourishing the next generation, we will regress into a pseudo-intimacy and get all caught up in our work or in gambling or our electronic toys and we will stagnate and die like spoiled children.

Jesus says that if we stay connected to him, if we stay in the "conscious contact" of Step Eleven, then we will be fruitful. It will happen. Step Twelve will naturally follow Eleven, but Twelve without Eleven is an empty gong, a clanging cymbal. Jesus tells us not to be concerned about carrying the message, about being fruitful in our service work. If we stay connected to him, to the vine, we will be fruitful whether we know it or not—and often it is better for our egos that we do not know it.

Jesus also reminds us that every branch that bears fruit must be pruned. If we continue on the steps of our recovery, we will be pruned. I call the Seventh Step the "pruning" step. If we humbly ask God to remove our shortcomings, God will, and we will not always like it. None of us *likes* to be pruned; all of us *need* to be pruned.

As I have mentioned, I am a city boy who had lawn jobs as a teenager and who pruned lots of bushes and trees without knowing what I was doing. I have had to observe and interview people much more knowledgeable than I about "pruning." I asked a religious brother who was in charge of the orchard at a retreat center in Toronto how he decided where to prune, and he simply gestured and said, "I prune where the tree is running into itself." I asked a couple in Mazeppa,

Minnesota who owned an apple orchard how they decided where to prune and they answered, "We prune to open the tree to the sun." Aren't those great responses for the way our higher power works with us in the Seventh Step, pruning us where we keep tripping ourselves up, and allowing us to open more to our higher power?

I find my recovery goes best when I bring one shortcoming at a time to God. Otherwise, I get confused and I am working with God on too many fronts to make real progress. In recent years, my Seventh Step work has been to ask God to help me ask on my own behalf; to ask God to help me be willing to receive from others; to ask God to remove my propensity to pack too much into too little time. At the moment my Seventh Step is asking God to remove my shortcoming of failing to invite God in at the beginning of any project, from driving to eating, from beginning a counseling session to beginning a round of golf. As I invite God in at the start of my activity, I find God wants to always be in conscious contact with me and that any activity is both easier and more enjoyable when I do it together with our higher power.

I agree with the clergyman who states in *Twelve Steps and Twelve Traditions* that Step Six is the step that separates the adults from the children in recovery. Whatever growth I have known has come largely from concentration on Steps Six and Seven. Step Seven is one of only two steps that has a prayer formally connected with it in *Alcoholics Anonymous*:

My Creator, I am now willing that you
    should have all of me, good
and bad. I pray that you now remove from me
    every single defect
of character which stands in the way of my usefulness
    to you and my

fellows. Grant me strength, as I go out from here,
   to do your bidding,
   Amen.

You are the vine; we are the branches. Prune us as you will for
the glory of God and the service of our brothers and sisters.
(**DR**)

Letting Go

"Receive the Holy Spirit. Whose sins you forgive are forgiven them...."
■ JOHN 20:22, 23

*If you have a resentment you want to be free of, if you will pray
for the person or thing that you resent, you will be free.*
■ *Alcoholics Anonymous*, PAGE 552

Michael Kennedy, a recently deceased priest and dear friend of mine, used to start virtually every homily with "I wasn't there, but others were; and they told others and they told others and eventually the word has come down to you and me." That is particularly pertinent with Pentecost, because in our Scriptures we have competing or companionable accounts of Pentecost, depending on how you look at the Bible. In John's gospel, Pentecost is Easter Sunday night. Jesus appears to the disciples, blesses them with the peace of His Spirit, and enables them to grant forgiveness in the name and the power of that Spirit. In John, Pentecost is all about the Spirit of forgiveness. In Luke/Acts, the account of Pentecost we are more used to, the Spirit of the risen Jesus descends on the disciples fifty days after the Resurrection in a manifestation of wind and tongues of fire. They are moved to mission, to speak boldly of the risen Jesus, and their listeners are all able to hear and understand them, each in their own language.

Which was the actual event? The best we can answer is

both because both are contained in our Scriptures. Both are true; both have lessons to teach.

Let's get a running start on those lessons. Pentecost was originally a harvest festival for the people living in the area the Israelites settled. They promptly added a historical dimension to the feast, celebrating on Pentecost their arrival at Sinai, the establishment of the Covenant, and the reception of the Law. So it was already a Jewish feast. Now with the risen Jesus' gift to us of the Spirit, it becomes a major Christian feast, actually the birthday of the community of Jesus as a Church.

In Luke/Acts that community is established virtually as a Step Twelve community, called to "carry the message to others," as they "speak about the marvels God has accomplished." In John, that community is established virtually as a Step Five community, called to let go of "resentments, fear, ego, and dishonesty," especially resentments. Jesus says: "Receive the Holy Spirit. Whose sins you forgive, they are forgiven."

We all know the importance from both *Alcoholics Anonymous* and from our own experience of letting go of resentments. On page 64 of *Alcoholics Anonymous* we read: "Resentment is the 'number one' offender. It destroys more alcoholics than anything else." Need I go on? *Alcoholics Anonymous* does contain the wonderful story about praying with our resentments, words so sacred that they appear on page 552 of every edition of the Big Book. "If you have a resentment you want to be free of, if you will pray for the person or the thing that you resent, you will be free...." I know the truth of those words from my own experience.

Other than that story, *Alcoholics Anonymous* is not so strong on the struggle involved in letting go of resentments or on exactly how to let go of them and what the consequences are. In the Pentecost Gospel Jesus knows how hard it is for us to forgive. He knows that the best we can do of ourselves is to get even or perhaps pretend to all that we have forgotten the offense. But forgiveness remembers and still lets go. And Jesus knows that only God can do that, so he gives us his Spirit in order that we might both acknowledge the hurt and let go of it, and forgive and trust that God will somehow work good through it, at least the good of humbling us.

Enough of resentments and forgiveness for now. The important point for us Christians and for us in recovery is that Pentecost is our birthday. We all know that the most important word of our recovery is the first word of the First Step—WE. This is a community program, not a solitary program; this is recovery, not sobriety that we are after. And so we have a home group; we sponsor and are sponsored; we are available for service because we are climbing the Steps together. An awesome speaker at a recent recovery round-up used the phrase: "Teamwork makes the dream work." Yes—the dream of our climbing all twelve of the Steps, the dream of recovery.

We also are here as Christians worshiping together because we know that the most important word for us Christians is also WE. Our discipleship is not Jesus and I. It is Jesus and we. Jesus did not call just one to be his follower. He called people in groups—Peter and James and John, Martha and Mary. And he continues to do the same today—Mary and Tom, and Steve and Ed, and Karen and Sandy, and….

Pentecost is our birthday. It is our opportunity to celebrate and give thanks that Jesus calls us to be a community that both forgives and receives forgiveness; a community that both receives the message and carries it; a community that brings our gifts to one another and shares and receives of those gifts; a community that celebrates the death and rising of Jesus every Sunday that we might celebrate that death and rising on Tuesday and on Friday; a community that listens to the Word on Sunday that we might hear that Word from our spouses and our sponsors and our children on Wednesday; a community that prays on Sunday to be aware of our brothers and sisters still in the ditch of alcoholism and addiction that we might be of service to them on Thursday.

We are that community, aren't we? We hope so; we pray so.

Happy Birthday! (DR)

Ordinary Time

Look the word "ordinary" up in the dictionary, and you'll find the following synonyms: "of no special quality or interest," "commonplace," and "unexceptional." Small wonder that few of us would want to be referred to as simply "ordinary"! Our culture expects us to be exceptional, interesting, or different. Maybe that's part of why a whole generation of people find unique tattoos so attractive—they're a visible form of personal distinctiveness.

But the ordinary doesn't have to be humdrum. There's something soothing about the familiar chair, the daily home routine, the morning cup of coffee. We have time to order ourselves. This is particularly true for those of us who have dealt with dysfunction and chaos in earlier chapters of our lives. We come to recognize that rather than being boring, ordinary times bring subtle changes that prove to be part of meaningful growth.

The liturgical year offers us two seasons of Ordinary Time, the first after Christmas, and the second after Easter. In winter, we hear a great deal about the life of Jesus and his ministry. We see him reaching out to people in comfort and in challenge. We hear the great sermons captured by the gospel writers. We see his intimate friendships and his unhesitating reach across boundaries that the Jews of his day considered inviolable. In summer and fall, inspired by the descent of the Holy Spirit at Pentecost, we turn our attention to how to be more effective disciples. This is Spirited time, Church time, our time, when we move, hopefully, as the Spirit-filled Body of Christ.

As people of recovery, we follow God during Ordinary Time with hearts open to our own growth and change. We seek greater wells of spiritual maturity and a focus that is increasingly outward—moving away from ourselves and increasingly toward loving and serving others.

So, if in winter's Ordinary Time we *learn* what Jesus does, in summer's Ordinary Time we walk and weed the rows of crops that have been planted, and learn how to *do* what Jesus does.

Ordinary Time, used well, is both consoling and rigorous. We arise each day to pray and meditate and receive the day's marching orders from our God. We do this because, as that great line from *Alcoholics Anonymous* puts it: "We have entered the world of the Spirit" (page 84). (TV)

Following More Closely

"What are you looking for?"

■ JOHN 1:38

*[O]ur Creator has entered into our hearts and lives
in a way which is indeed miraculous.*

■ *Alcoholics Anonymous*, PAGE 25

With the onset of Ordinary Time, we say goodbye to the out-of-the-ordinary and hello to the routine. Yet it is in our ordinary routine that we truly live out our recovery and our spirituality. As St. Francis de Sales stated, "Pray God that we might do the ordinary extraordinarily well."

Ordinary Time offers us a passage from the Gospel of John that reminds us of why we are here at all—"to come and see," to come and see who this Jesus is and what he might have to offer us. We are basically praying for an intimate knowledge of our caring God as manifested in Jesus, that we might love him more and follow him more closely.

Today our following of Jesus starts with his asking us perhaps the most difficult question a human can be asked: "What do you want? What are you looking for?"

How remarkable Jesus is with us! He does not presume to know what we want nor does he tell us what we want. "What do you want?" and he waits for our answer. The best we can do is "Where do you live?" Okay, says Jesus, if that is what you want, I will show you. He can only come to us where we are, not where he or we would prefer we be. Jesus knows that we have desires, longings for what we do not yet have or for what we yet are not. Human himself, he must have known desire and so he can presume that we have desires as well. Jesus wants people of desire, people who know they are not complete, who do not act as though they have it all. He loves our incompleteness because he knows that only God can complete us and hopes and prays we will acknowledge that as well.

How congruent all of this is with *Alcoholics Anonymous* ("The Big Book"):

I could expound on page 25: "The central fact of our lives today is the absolute certainty that our Creator has entered into our hearts and lives in a way which is indeed miraculous. He has commenced to accomplish those things for us which we could never do by ourselves"—but I won't.

I could wax eloquently on page 46: "As soon as we admitted the possible existence of a Creative Intelligence, a Spirit of the Universe underlying the totality of things, we began to be possessed of a new sense of power and direction"—but I won't.

Instead I will linger with these words from page 55:

> ... deep down in every man, woman, and child, is the fundamental idea of God. It may be obscured by calamity, by pomp, by worship of other things, but in some form or other it is there. For faith in a Power greater than ourselves, and miraculous demonstrations of that power in human lives, are facts as old as humans themselves....

We all have that God-hole, that empty space, that we have

been trying to fill with everything imaginable. The more we try to fill it, the bigger the hole gets and the emptier we are. Once we let the hole be there, once we surrender, then God can day by day fill the hole until God fills it completely by union with us at the end.

Remarkably similar to today's gospel, page 55 of *Alcoholics Anonymous* continues: "If our testimony helps sweep away prejudice, enables you to think honestly, encourages you to search diligently within yourself, then, if you wish, you can join us on the Broad Highway."

What an invitation! What great Twelfth-Stepping: "carrying the message to others." It is just like what Andrew does in today's gospel. He has found someone who is not prejudiced, who is honest and encouraging. His name is Jesus. And he goes running to his brother Simon and shares his experience, strength, and hope. Simon Peter joins him and the rest is history. (DR)

Mary as our Model

When the wine ran short, the mother of Jesus said to him,
"They have no wine." And Jesus said to her, "Woman, how does your
concern affect me? My hour has not yet come." His mother said to the
servers, "Do whatever he tells you." ■ JOHN 2:3–5

Then, in A.A., we looked and listened. Everywhere we saw failure
and misery transformed by humility into priceless assets. We heard
story after story of how humility had brought strength out of weakness.
In every case, pain had been the price of admission into a new life.
But this admission price had purchased more than we expected.
It brought a measure of humility, which we soon discovered to be
a healer of pain. We began to fear pain less, and desire humility more
than ever. ■ *Twelve Steps and Twelve Traditions*, STEP SEVEN, P. 75

As you may know, Catholics hold Mary the Mother of Jesus with a particular love and reverence. She is central to Catholic piety all over the globe, particularly in the country from which my spiritual roots spring, Ireland. My Irish grandmothers, Margaret and Hanorah, had a deep attachment to the Blessed Mother.

In addition to praying the Rosary, at the end of the day my grandmothers would say their evening prayers using prayer cards. I remember sitting with them as a child, fascinated. Most of the cards featured beautiful traditional images of Mary. Some depicted the mother of the angelic, cherubic

Jesus, a woman serene and beautiful, embracing her infant. Others showed Mary as the Queen of Heaven, her arms outstretched, her eyes raised to God, the picture of holiness.

They were beautiful images. But the Scriptures provide additional vivid images of Mary. She was a real woman, with the concerns of real women, as we see in her role as a guest at the wedding in Cana. Here we see many dimensions of Mary—Mary the observer, Mary the busybody, Mary the outspoken. I like this Mary!

In some ways, she strikes me as a typical mother. She sees a need—in this case, a need for hospitality and welcome. And then she thinks, "My son can take care of that." So she makes her pointed comment: "They have no wine." And even though Jesus gets a little peeved that she's putting him on the spot, even though he claims he's not ready to act, Mary knows he's going to address the need. So she turns to those serving and with confidence says, "Do whatever he tells you."

One of the things I find fascinating about Mary and her actions is that she is not blaming or criticizing anyone, even though in her culture it would have been a scandalous lapse of hospitality to run out of wine. We don't hear her coming from "there's something wrong." Instead, she seems to be focused on what's missing. "They have no wine." And she trusts that when Jesus is asked to help those around fill the gap, he will.

Seeing the world with the eyes of Mary, looking for what's missing, not what's wrong, and then inviting God and others in to remedy the situation is something that every disciple of Jesus can do. It's also a muscle that gets well trained when we work our spiritual program, particularly when we work Steps Six and Seven.

When I first started working the program, I was very put off by the constant use of the word humility. I had had enough humiliation, thank you. I didn't realize that there was a difference between the two words, a difference that I have come to cherish. I have come to see that humiliation, which results from a shame-filled defeat, is very different from surrendering my pride and having the willingness to look and see where I need to change and grow. To live life humbly, I have to first see what needs to be different (which I do in the Fourth and Fifth Steps) and then be willing to have God work those needed changes in me (through the Sixth and Seventh Steps). I must take an honest look, as Mary did, and see what is missing. Only then can I, like Mary, invite a power greater than myself to provide the needed healing or change.

In my life, sponsorship is a structure for inviting this sort of clarity. When I bring an issue to my sponsor, I work to stay open to hear what action she thinks would be fruitful. I then can take that suggestion to my prayer. Sometimes, I have to pray to be willing to take the suggestion. Or even to "be willing to be willing!"

Similarly, I am called as a Christian and a committed member of the fellowship, to be watchful wherever I am for those "they have no wine" moments. Some of the moments will be big. I only have to look at my local paper to see major issues, local and global, that can be served by my humble action. Some moments will be small. I might find myself taking time to linger after a meeting to reach out to someone who is struggling with an issue or still suffering from the consequences of addiction.

Sometimes this is easy, and sometimes it's very challenging. When we see the "no wine" moments in our families, our faith communities, our groups, we stand at a crossroads. Do we just move along, live with dimmer vision, or do we, like Mary, tell the truth about what we see, and take our concerns to Jesus and to action?

I know the prayer that my Irish grandmothers would pray

for us: "Holy Mary, mother of God, pray for us…" Pray for us that we might look with open eyes, and speak with a courageous voice. Pray for us that together, we will follow your son more fully. Amen. (**TV**)

Giving and Receiving

*A leper came to him and kneeling down begged him and said,
"If you wish, you can make me clean." Moved with pity, he stretched
out his hand, touched him, and said to him, "I do will it. Be made
clean." The leprosy left him immediately, and he was made clean.*

■ MATTHEW 8:1–3

*"My Creator, I am now willing that you should have all of me,
good and bad. I pray that you now remove from me every single defect
of character which stands in the way of my usefulness to you and my
fellows. Grant me strength, as I go out from here, to do your bidding.
Amen."* ■ *Alcoholics Anonymous*, THE SEVENTH STEP PRAYER, PAGE 76

For a time, I had the privilege of working as a chaplain in a
large medical center. Day in and day out, I saw people struggle with really dire diagnoses. I sat with young mothers facing the removal of brain tumors. I sat with senior citizens
who were facing disfiguring laryngectomies. I sat with teen-
agers and college-aged youth who were hooked up to dozens
of electrodes trying to diagnose serious seizure disorders.

There was a young woman on my floor who requested
the chaplain early one morning. I looked at her chart and
discovered that she was recovering from a serious operation
on her brain that had not gone well. The hoped-for outcome
had not happened.

I knocked on her door and poked my head in, saying,

"Good morning, I'm Trish; I'm the chaplain." I was very startled by the fact that the room was almost completely dark. The blinds were closed by heavy curtains; the room pitch black except for a little light coming from the fixture over the bed. In the room were the patient and her partner seated in the chair next to her bed.

I sat down and said to the patient, "I know you wanted a visit from the chaplain; how are you doing?" And she just stared at me. And her look was one of great pain, certainly physical pain, but she also seemed to me to be in very deep emotional pain. And there was silence, and I said, "Would you like to talk about it?" And there was silence. And her partner leaned over and said to me, "You know, because of the surgery, she isn't able to talk right now." And I said, "Oh, okay, I see."

I sat for another moment of silence. And I thought to myself, "However am I going to minister to this woman? She wants the chaplain but she can't speak." So I just started talking a little bit, and I felt very awkward because I just didn't know what to do. So I ended up saying, "You know, maybe it would be better if I came back tomorrow, when you're feeling a little better, and we could speak then." And she looked at me very intensely and she shook her head strongly back and forth, "No." I said, "So you want me to stay?" And she very calmly nodded her head "Yes." And I sat there. And I was really at a loss.

And then I remembered: This patient is Catholic. And because I am Catholic, in the morning, I would go to the sacristy in the chapel and carry the Eucharist with me. So I said to her, "Do you think that you would like to receive the Eucharist?" Her eyes widened and she gave a very strong nod, "Yes," and her companion said, "Oh, that would mean so much to us...," and told me about the love they feel in their faith community and what the Eucharist meant in both their lives.

So I took out the bedside ritual, and we read the Scripture, and we said the prayer, and we prayed the words that Jesus gave us. And then I took a consecrated host and held it up to her saying those familiar words: "The Body of Christ." For the first time in that morning, I heard her voice: she whispered "Amen." She took the host, and placed it on her tongue, and she closed her eyes. And a look of great serenity came over her face. She opened her eyes, reached out and squeezed her beloved's hand, looked up at me, and smiled.

Suddenly that room that seemed so dark, so full of pain, and so lacking in hope, had a presence of peace. The three of us were still sitting together in the silence, but something had changed in that room. It was no longer a silence of no words. It was a silence of every word, every loving word of promise and grace made to us by God, a silence of Christ's healing presence with us. And I knew, maybe in a way I never had before, that where two or more gather in his name, Christ is there. The patient's physical body was not different because of that Eucharist. But I believe that healing happened.

One of the most wonderful things about this story is that it reminds us how we get to come to Jesus: We get to come as we are, imperfect. We don't bring whole selves to Jesus any more than the patient I met or the leper of Jesus' day. We bring broken selves. Many of us, as we hit our bottoms or stayed alongside someone we loved who was going down the drain, felt like lepers. We were filled with shame and remorse. Our reserves of hope were exhausted. Like the leper, the consequences of addiction made us feel exiled from everything we held most dear.

When we took the first three steps, we took our desperate need for healing to the God of our understanding. We embraced the transformation available in the Steps and the supportive presence of those in the program. As we continue walking the path of recovery, we go on bringing our need for healing to our Higher Power both in the rooms and through the practices of our faith. No matter where we are, like the leper, we come to God. We bring our crabby selves. We bring our stressed-out-about-work selves. We bring our in-a-marital-crisis selves. We bring our feeling-like-we-have no-friends selves. We bring our fearful-of-the-future selves. We bring our feeling-lost-and-forgotten selves to God, particularly when we come to his table. What do we find there? "Real presence." What do we find in the rooms? "Real presence."

"You can heal me if you wish," declares the leper. Can we come to Jesus today with the same conviction and belief that the leper had on that day a long, long time ago? Can we say today, with hope and faith, "Only say the word, and I shall be healed?" And listen for the answer that always awaits us, particularly when we "give ourselves to this simple program": "I will do it." (TV)

Giving Back to God

"Show me the coin that pays the census tax."
Then they handed him the Roman coin. He said to them,
"Whose image is this and whose inscription?" They replied, "Caesar's."
At that he said to them, "Then repay to Caesar what belongs to Caesar
and to God what belongs to God." ■ MATTHEW 22:20–21

Half measures availed us nothing. We stood at the turning point.
We asked His protection and care with complete abandon.

■ *Alcoholics Anonymous*, PAGE 59

My oldest child was like a lot of first babies. She took her good, sweet time getting born. By the time she arrived, I was absolutely knocked-down, dragged-out tired. So when the nurse came over and laid a swaddled little bundle down in the crook of my arm, I embraced her in a sort of matter-of-fact state of exhaustion that bordered on a coma.

I looked at her and thought: "Is this my baby?" I took a really close look. "This baby looks exactly like my husband. This must be my baby." And in that moment of recognition, of seeing the glimmer of another face that I love so, imprinted so distinctly on this beautiful little baby, I was swept away on a river of aliveness and love. All my exhaustion seemed to fall away and I was filled with excitement—all because I recognized something in an image.

Being inspired to action by an image is at the heart of today's gospel. In this story, we hear yet again of the hostility Jesus faced. A set of unlikely partners steps forward to try to entrap him around the question of paying taxes to Caesar: "some of the Pharisees and some of the Herodians."

One of the strange things about this story is the fact that the Pharisees, those deeply pious and religious purists, would team up with the Herodians. The Herodians, as their name implies, were partisans of the ruling Roman family. They were a group of Jews who had compromised their faith and piety, in order to win favors from the governing forces. The Pharisees and the Herodians made strange partners in their attempt to discredit Jesus, because they despised each other.

After some sweet-talking flattery, we come to the question. "Is it lawful to pay taxes to the emperor, or not?" If Jesus answered "No," the Herodians, those who enjoyed the benefits of Roman rule, would report him to the authorities as a traitor or seditionist. If Jesus answered "Yes," the Pharisees would have ample fuel to discredit him among the people as a Roman sympathizer, a person unfaithful to the faith of Israel.

Now, as we know, Jesus outwits them. But he does so in an absolutely stunning move. He uses the coin itself, a coin that was so offensive to many Jews that they refused to even carry it. On one side appeared the bust of Tiberius wearing the laurel wreath, a sign of his divinity. The legend beneath it read, "Emperor Tiberius, august son of the august God." On the other side, his title *Pontifex maximus*, high priest, appears. The coin was a universal sign and statement of the worship and power of the emperor in Christ's time. And the Jews refused to worship the emperor.

It's within that complex political context that Jesus answers them. "Why put me to the test? Bring me a coin." We can only imagine the agony of this moment as this occupied people are forced to pull out this incredibly offensive coin to answer the question, "Whose image and inscription is this?" "Caesar's," is their reply—in one word, an expression of the despair of the nation. Then comes Jesus' stunning response: "Render unto Caesar what is Caesar's, and give to God what is God's."

"Give to God what is God's" invites us to the next logical if unspoken question. If we are to give to God what is God's, then what is God's? The Pharisees, the Herodians, the Zealots, and all of us are left with the challenge of answering that question.

Jesus hints at where we'll find the answer. He holds the denarius and says, here is Caesar's image: Give Caesar the thing that has his image on it. And what has God's image on it? The book of Genesis tells us the answer: God says, "Let us make humankind in our image, after our likeness...." We are the image of God, every last one of us. And all of creation is covered over with God's fingerprints. It has all come from God, and it is all going to God, and humankind was given the astonishing, magnificent task of stewarding this creation.

What is most subversive in Jesus' answer is that there is nothing, really, ultimately, that is Caesar's. It is all God's. To answer Jesus' call to give to God what is God's is to respond with the gift of our entire being, all that we are, and everything in creation that is entrusted to us. Giving God what is God's involves the decisions we make, the resources we distribute, the service we do, the praise we give.

I've often thought that those of us who have received the gift of the Steps have been given a tremendous edge in doing this. Our First and Second Steps force us to look at the fact that we are, in so very many ways, powerless. And then we receive the Third Step's amazing invitation to surrender. We can make a decision, an active choice, "to turn our will and our lives over to the care of God as we understood God." We also know that when we consciously work the Sixth Step, we are "sincerely trying to grow in the image and likeness" (*Twelve Steps and Twelve Traditions*, p. 63) of our Creator. We have been given an amazing structure in which we can "give to God what is God's."

The journey of letting go, growing in God's image and giving ourselves fully to a power greater than ourselves, is a lifetime process. Although I recognize that it takes time, knowing it is happening is a source of hope to me. I told you about that moment of recognition, that flood of love I felt for Nora the night she was born. I can only begin to imagine what God must feel when God looks at each one of us and sees the divine image reflected—and God's even greater joy when we freely give ourselves to one another in service of his will. (TV)

Prayer and Praying

*Rising very early before dawn, Jesus left and went off
to a deserted place, where he prayed.* ■ MARK 1:29

*Our real purpose is to fit ourselves to be of maximum service to God
and the people about us.* ■ *Alcoholics Anonymous*, PAGE 77

Today's gospel picks right up from Jesus teaching with authority. After Jesus drives out the demon, he goes on to heal
all whom he touches. Those healings do not prove anything;
they simply manifest the power of God that is present. Jesus
does not move simply as a wonderworker; he has come to
proclaim the love of God for us all right here, right now. The
people are gaga about the cures; they miss the deeper message. That is a primary reason why Jesus must move on.

In a sense, this day in the life of Jesus, with its healings and
preachings, sounds so remarkable. Yet, really, it is similar to
your day and mine. We speak and act and touch and everyone
around us is invited to get either healthier or sicker depending on the quality of our presence. A day in the life of Jesus
is no more whole or holy than a day in the life of you or me
can be. Let us remember how sacred this day is.

But here is the line that I want to linger with: "Jesus went
off…and prayed." That is a remarkable sentence on at least
two levels. First of all, I submit, most of us, if we even consider or contemplate Jesus, treat him as divine and not as hu-

man. That shows because we never invite him into the situations of our human lives before we enter those situations. With this gospel in mind, I carefully and intentionally did that this past week. One day I asked the Spirit to be with me as I met with a person I find difficult. I actually enjoyed the conversation. I asked the Spirit to be with me that I might lovingly and yet definitely confront one of the guests at a treatment center, who seemed to me to be just wasting time. I spoke loving and direct truth to him and he cried and finally began to do a Third Step. I asked the Spirit to be with us all at our First Wednesday gathering as I felt shallow in my preparations, and I was given two questions to ask those of us who were there: "When have you been well loved and what was involved?" And "When have you loved well and what was involved?" And it was one of the deeper meetings I have been to recently. Those were just a few instances in a week of small miracles, all because I paused beforehand and asked the Spirit of our Higher Power to be with me.

There is a second level to the statement that "Jesus prayed" that deserves even more exploration. Jesus certainly had the mindset of a Twelve-Stepper when you consider that remarkable sentence on page 77 of *Alcoholics Anonymous*: "Our real purpose is to fit ourselves to be of maximum service to God and the people about us." As our recovery deepens, that becomes the purpose of our lives. Eight pages later, after we have made our way through the thicket of amends and the commitment to a continued inventory that is Step Ten, we get to this:

> Much has already been said about receiving strength,
> inspiration, and direction from Him who has all
> knowledge and power. If we have carefully followed
> directions, we have begun to sense the flow of His Spirit
> into us. To some extent we have become God-conscious.

We have begun to develop this vital sixth sense. But we must go further and that means more action.

Step Eleven suggests prayer and meditation…

And then *Alcoholics Anonymous* proceeds to lead us through one way of praying in the morning:

On awakening, let us think about the twenty-four hours ahead….We ask God to direct our thinking….We ask God for inspiration, an intuitive thought or a decision…We usually conclude the period of meditation with a prayer that we be shown all though the day what our next step is to be…. (pages 86 and 87)

That is so similar to the way that Jesus must have prayed in today's gospel, seeking direction and the courage to follow it. He could so easily have followed his ego and settled in as a wonderworker and miracle doer, and yet his mission was to proclaim the Love of God for us right here, right now, just as we are; and so he had to be about it and he moved on.

Jesus Christ prayed; Jesus Christ listened for the direction of his Father and our Father. You and I are called to pray if we are going to get serious about our recovery. Our illness is primarily spiritual and our recovery must be primarily spiritual. I recently did an inventory of some of the current popular Christian books on prayer and I was quite impressed by all the ways they try to invite us, even seduce us to pray. They contain phrases like these:

Prayer is revolution.
Prayer is encounter.
To pray is to change.
Prayer is compassion.

All well and good, but I prayed this morning and I am praying with you, simply because I am not God, but a creature held in the hands of a caring God. I pray because I cannot ward off suffering; I pray because I cannot protect myself or loved ones as I would like; I pray because I cannot effect as I would want, with the success I would like; I pray because I cannot secure the future and because I do not have clarity as to my next step.

It sounds so weak and yet I find it relates me profoundly with you, because you cannot do any of those things either, nor do you know the future, nor do you have clarity. And I find it relates me profoundly with the living God, and I become ever more patient and content to wait for God to act in God's good time and mine—as God always does.

We pray because we are not God. A seeker once sought out a swami by the shores of the Ganges in India and asked him to teach the seeker how to pray. The swami took the man to the water, asked him to kneel down, and then held the man's head under water. When the man finally shook himself free, he turned to the swami and asked him what that was all about. "When you want to pray as much as you want to breathe, then come back."

Well, we are back and we are at prayer today and we are breathing today. May the same be true tomorrow. (**DR**)

Being Restored

*"Which is easier, to say to the paralytic, 'Your sins are forgiven,'
or to say, 'Rise, pick up your mat and walk'?"* ■ MARK 2:9-12

*Provided you hold back nothing, your sense of relief will mount
from minute to minute. The dammed-up emotions of years break
out of their confinement, and miraculously vanish as soon as they are
exposed. As the pain subsides, a healing tranquility takes its place.
And when humility and serenity are so combined, something else
of great moment is apt to occur.*

■ *Twelve Steps and Twelve Traditions*, PAGE 62

My friend Kwame and I were sharing with one another our
earliest memories of hearing about God. Kwame is from
Ghana, and he told me that the very first story he remembers
hearing about God was the great creation story that is told by
many West African peoples.

When the earth was made, the story goes, God was very
close to humanity. God and humankind lived close to one
another, so close that you just had to reach up your hand and
you could touch and feel God. But there was an old woman
who was constantly working, pounding cassava root to make
fufu, one of the mainstays of the West African diet. She was
using a mortar and a very long pestle, and every time she
pounded it, as she worked and worked, she hit God in the
eye. God got tired of being poked in the eye, and so God

moved further and further away from humanity, and went into the skies.

As Christians, we also recognize that our actions can put space between us and God, but we understand it in a different way. We don't believe that anything we do pushes God away. But we do believe that there are things we do that move us away from God. We call those things sin. Some of those sins are individual, some of them are communal. In the program, we speak of "character defects" and "derelictions," but also of "sins."

I'm not sure why, but we live in an age where people don't like the idea of sin. Perhaps because in times not too long past there was such a burdensome overemphasis on it, accompanied by fear of damnation and hell. In the program, we have the opportunity to develop a healthy ability to recognize our imperfections and work on them, a process of building character.

In the program, we come to see that it is God who makes the healing changes that are needed in us when we are ready, willing, and receptive partners. We can see a pattern for how this happens in the gospel story of the healing of the paralytic person. Let's consider what the gospel has just told us about it by looking at three actors in our sacred story: the paralytic, the stretcher-bearers, and, of course, Jesus. Each of these tells us something essential about returning to God for healing and forgiveness.

First the paralytic. We don't know much about this person other than that he is male and paralyzed. No age is given; Jesus refers to him as "child." What can we learn from this person about bringing ourselves to God? One thing might be surrender; the act of admitting something is not working, admitting that we are in need. What do I need to bring to God? Where am I at a standstill with God or other human beings?

Stuck? What is immobilizing me? Are there obstacles, made by myself or others, that have to be broken through so that I can be healed and made whole?

Another might be recognizing our powerlessness. The person in our story is paralyzed; he can't do what he needs to do by himself. Like him, we need help, sometimes extreme help; help from God and help from one another. One of the most striking things about this story is that the person on the stretcher cannot get to Jesus by himself. He needs to be borne to Jesus by others, and he has the faith and willingness to ask for help. What do we learn from this second set of actors? What do the stretcher-bearers say to us about God's love and forgiveness?

Think about how bold these actors in the story are. They are so committed to bring their friend that they will not let the obstacle of the obstructed door stop them. It is a demonstration of great love and also great faith that they will go to any lengths to support the paralytic. They go up to the roof, and begin the incredible task of literally digging through the clay ceiling of that house. There is no mention of being concerned about risking the anger of the residents or the disapproval of the community.

What does it mean to be someone who is so committed to the well-being of another that we will defy convention? To what lengths would we be willing to go to take those in need to the arms of Christ? Whether that is personal healing or systemic change, have we been willing to place ourselves in the position of another person, share their reality, and transform it? The stretcher-bearers remind us that what we cannot do alone, we can do in the power of community, by reaching out our hand for help, and by grasping the hands of others. Perhaps some of the brokenness we bring to God has to do with the things that have stopped us from truly helping others.

It is the faith of the Church and the belief of the recovering community that when we come to God for forgiveness and healing, God will respond. And we don't come to God alone. We come in community, either through the sacrament of reconciliation or in our Fifth Step.

My friend Nicanor told me a beautiful story about the *Rito de Perdón*, a ritual of reconciliation done by people in the small mountain hamlets of the Andes. These towns are very small; there might be only forty or fifty people in the community. And because the towns are small and isolated, the people have a deep sense of being dependent upon one another. Whenever there is a break in relationship—whenever something has gone awry and harmony is not present—any person can call the entire community together for the *Rito de Perdón*. How this works is that every person in the town lines up in a great circle. One by one, the people go past each other, and each one asks every single other person for forgiveness, a forgiveness that is empowered by their faith in God. The priest is included in this ritual. And by the time all have gone to each other, there are often many tears of gratitude; a sense of healing; and most of all a sense that they have moved back closer to God.

The last powerful actor in this story is Jesus, the one who demonstrates what we'll find when we seek out God's love and healing. There he sits in the house, utterly unsurprised by the wild activity going on around him. They lower the person down, and without a moment's hesitation, Jesus says to him, with a term of endearment, "Child, your sins are forgiven." No pause and no reluctance. Here you are, you who have come to me with such great faith: You are forgiven.

That is what is both startling and wondrous about Jesus: That this person's sins are removed. That he is restored to wholeness. Why? Not because he asks, not because his friends or family ask, but simply because they have come to Jesus in faith. They come, and he responds. That is the astonishing generosity and willingness of our God. This God that will do for us what we cannot do for ourselves, if only we come to God, openhearted and willing. (TV)

Watching Our Words

"A good person out of the store of goodness in his heart produces good, but an evil person out of a store of evil produces evil; for from the fullness of the heart the mouth speaks." ■ LUKE 6:39–45

Nothing pays off like restraint of tongue and pen.

■ STEP TEN, *Twelve Steps and Twelve Traditions*

Researchers tell us that from the first "good morning" to the last good night, we each speak between 25,000 and 30,000 words a day—enough words to fill a 50-page book every 24 hours! Add it up and you discover that the average person spends about fifteen years, or about one-fifth of his or her life, talking!

"From the fullness of the heart the mouth speaks," says Jesus in this gospel story. Which leaves me wondering: How many of those many words do I speak from the fullness of the heart? What am I saying each day with my 25,000 or 30,000 words—and what do those words say about me?

Do my words calm? Do they heal? Do they build people up? Do they tear them down? Do they hurt? Do they comfort? Do they hide the truth? Do they reveal the truth? Just looking at that brief list alone, I'm humbled by the power of words, particularly since I know that I am often fairly automatic in my speaking, not giving it all that much thought.

A few years ago, my daughter told me about a visit Officer

Randy, the police liaison with our city's elementary schools, made to her class. While speaking with the second graders, Officer Randy mentioned a saying that grownups say to kids a lot—often when they are trying to help children deal with hurtful comments. It's the familiar phrase, "Sticks and stones will break my bones but names will never hurt me." Officer Randy told the kids that he didn't think that that saying was true at all. He said that when he talks to grownups about when they were kids, often the thing that's hardest for them to forget are the words that hurt them, such as names they were called or putdowns by friends, family members, or classmates. He observed with the children that when people remember those things, they often feel hurt all over again.

Jesus describes our speech and our actions as being like "fruit." I think he's usually pretty intentional about the descriptions he chooses, so what does this comparison to fruit say to us? Well, for one thing, fruit doesn't appear overnight. Fruit comes as the end result of many things—watering, feeding, maybe some insect repellent, lots of sunlight, time for growth. The quality of the fruit is a testament to the long-term care the tree has received.

In the same way, Jesus tells us that our speech and our actions will reflect the care we have given our souls over time. And if we haven't given ourselves much care, the words we speak will be hollow at best and hurtful at worst. They won't be much more than "cheap talk," as we say. Do you know that just about every culture has a saying for "cheap talk"? In Swahili, it's *maneno matupu*, which means empty words.

Jesus didn't seem to have many empty words to say. And he did an awful lot of talking.

Jesus spoke things that no one had ever considered before—radical messages of love, intimate declarations about God, specific statements about justice. Jesus started a very new, very powerful conversation among human beings. The idea of Jesus being the source of a radical new conversation shouldn't surprise us in the least—don't we say that the "Word of God was made flesh, and dwelt among us?" And Jesus' talk was only made more powerful by the fact that he lived a life that was in complete alignment with his speaking. He walked his talk, as they say.

As recovering people, we are invited to practices of honesty, self-restraint, and integrity. We know the difference between the person who is quick to spout platitudes they've heard in the rooms and the person who is sharing their own experience, strength, and hope. Through self-examination, we come to watch our words carefully. In *Twelve Steps and Twelve Traditions*, we are reminded about the importance of self-restraint—in Step Ten, we are warned against righteous anger, teaching someone "a lesson," and the sly ways constructive criticism can camouflage what is really anger. "Nothing pays off like restraint of tongue and pen," we're told.

Our program and this gospel invite us to a new level of self-awareness, and there are some practices that improve our capacity.

One of them is to practice pausing before we say anything. Dr. Richard Carlson, the author of *Don't Sweat the Small Stuff (and it's all small stuff)*, advises "breathe before you speak." This simple strategy, he says has remarkable results including increased patience and a side benefit of more gratitude and respect from others. Taking that advice one step further, as Christians we could imagine that in that moment we are breathing in the spirit of God before we exhale our words.

Another idea comes from *At Home with the Word*, a publication that explores each Sunday's Scripture readings. It suggests that we might bring the practice of fasting, an ancient spiritual discipline, to our words. "Take stock of your own conversation in the coming days. Fast from words of anger; the curse hurled at another driver on the road, the sharp tone used with a spouse or child." That's a wonderful twist, I think, on an ancient practice.

And finally, we can reflect on how many of our up to 30,000 words a day are *maneno matupu*, empty words, and how many are life-giving. We can do that as people sharing the countless gifts of recovery in the program, and also as people who are part of keeping the conversation of Jesus alive in word and in action in the world. Perhaps we can find a way to make even 30 more words—.1% of the words we speak—count a little bit more today. (TV)

Our Caring God

When Jesus disembarked and saw the vast crowd,
his heart was moved with pity for them. ■ MARK 6:33

We made a decision to turn our will and our lives over to the CARE
of God, as we understood God. ■ *Alcoholics Anonymous,* PAGE 59

Our American English language struggles for an appropriate word to express the feelings, the empathy, Jesus experienced when he saw the crowd milling about like unguided sheep. The Greek original is *splangthei,* which means "to feel in one's bowels, in one's guts with the other person." It does not mean pity as we mean the word, which has a note of condescension from a superior person to a lesser one. It means "empathy" or "compassion" squared. Jesus ached with the people. He was angry with them that their shepherds were not really interested in nourishing them. His teaching and, soon, his feeding of the people, did not come from on high, but from the depths of his identification with the people. He spoke with authority because he shared his experience, strength, and hope in God and in life and also shared from a position of equality and mutuality with those he was speaking with.

I am digging as deeply as I can into this because it is so important for us Christians if we are really going to throw in our lot with Jesus and so important for us in recovery if we are going to fully climb the Third Step.

In Step Three, we turn our will and our lives over to the *care* of God, not just *to* God. How and why was Bill W. inspired to add the word *care* in fashioning the Third Step? I have called the reference librarian at AA International; I have googled *care and twelve steps*. I have come up with nothing. The only real piece I found from our early history was from the "Recovery Realm" message forums:

> For example, it is Saturday night and you and your
> spouse are going out for the night. You do not turn your
> child over to a babysitter—you turn your child over to
> the care of a babysitter, to watch and to guide. When we
> turn our will and lives over to the care of God, we do this
> not to become robots or carbon copies of each other but
> to let the higher power of our understanding watch and
> guide our will and our lives.

When I found nothing in Twelve-Step literature as to the origin or meaning of *care*, I went back to a piece I had read thirty years ago by the spiritual writer Henri Nouwen.

To appreciate what he and I and, I think, Bill W. are getting at, ask yourself right now:

- Who is your Higher Power? Perhaps, what is the image of God that is yours today?

- What is the expression on the face of your Higher Power as your Higher Power relates to you? Is your God sitting in judgment, waiting to reward you if you succeed and punish you if you fail?

Write this down—*The only God worth worshiping is a God that we in no way can control, a God who cares for us when we are*

good and when we are bad, a God who is always smiling on us.
As Nouwen wrote and as I concur, *caring* is not curing, fixing, making all better, or healing from a distance, or even taking care of someone—these all imply dealing with someone from a distance or from a superior position.

The word *care* has its linguistic roots in the Gothic word *kara*, which means to lament with, to grieve with, to cry out with, to ache with. To care means, first of all, "I am with you in what you are going through as much as one being can be with another. I want to enter with you into your pain or your joy before you and I do anything about it."

Who are our deepest friends, who mean most to us? Those who have offered advice or solutions and gone on their merry way or those who have said, "I am not sure either how you are to proceed but I will be with you as you take your next steps," and then have stuck around us as we make our decisions?

Our caring God does not cure from a distance, but heals up close; does not run away but runs toward us; does not get busy but gets quiet and close to us in both our pain and in our joy. Our caring God was with my friend Jim as he died of his cancer peacefully and surrounded by a loving family, and is with Jim's sister Patricia as her doctors have found a way to hold off her cancer. Which one has God cared for? Which one is the recipient of a miracle? Both! As Einstein said, either everything is a miracle or nothing is.

I apologize to you in the names of all of those well-meaning, often deeply religious people (myself included) who have preached to us of a God that has been either demanding or distant, judging or manipulating. Such folks were most often telling us of the God they had been taught to believe in or had projected in an attempt to control God and their eternal destiny. Let us forgive such teachers and move on.

If you just start saying "Thank you" for everything that you know you did not produce and direct—like that last breath, like that compliment you gave your spouse or child, like your honesty today—if you just start saying "Thank you," you are being opened to the caring God of the Third Step.

And how do we become a community that embodies this care of God for each other? Every time we ask someone to sponsor us or say yes to someone who asks us to sponsor him or her, we are embodying that care. Every time we make the coffee for our home group or are willing to serve a time as trusted servant, we are embodying that care. Every time we call another who has been absent for a time, we are embodying that care.

Every time... every time.... every time... you fill in the blanks.

The story is told of the central Minnesota farmer who went to the Benedictine monastery at St. John's in Collegeville that he might learn how to care for others. The host monk served him coffee to welcome him to the guest house; he poured the cup full and then kept on pouring. The farmer cried out in alarm. "You are so much like this cup, and so much like me," said the monk. "You see, we cannot be taught to care for others when we are so full of ourselves and of our opinion of ourselves. When the cup is empty, it can be filled. When we are empty of ourselves, we can be taught to care for others."

The only God worth worshiping has emptied his own cup (Philippians 2:6–11) and come to care for us. May we so experience that God that we are willing to empty our own cups and so care even more deeply for one another. (DR)

Surprising Sources

*"Which of these three, in your opinion, was neighbor to the robbers'
victim?" He answered, "The one who treated him with mercy."
Jesus said to him, "Go and do likewise."* ■ LUKE 10:29–37

*Life will take on new meaning. To watch people recover, to see them
help others, to watch loneliness vanish, to see a fellowship grow up
about you, to have a host of friends—this is an experience you must
not miss. We know you will not want to miss it. Frequent contact
with newcomers and with each other is the bright spot of our lives.*

■ STEP TWELVE, *Twelve Steps and Twelve Traditions*

The story of the Good Samaritan is one of the best known,
most familiar stories of Jesus. It's so familiar that many of us,
from the youngest to the oldest, could recite it with tremendous fidelity to Luke's text. We may also be familiar with a particular interpretation of this story. It goes something like this:

The priest and the Levite, the two characters that pass the
beaten man are Sadducees, in Jesus' day the most strict inter-
preters of the Torah. They hurry by the victim, in adherence
to the law, because even to approach the body would leave
them ritually impure and unable to perform their duties.
Then, along comes a Samaritan who shows the man mercy,
despite the fact that like the Sadducees he would have been
ritually unclean because of his act. The Samaritan's actions
are not limited by the parameters of the law. Answering to a

higher authority, he transcends the legalism of Judaism.

Now the problem with this interpretation is that it is incomplete, and it's incomplete in at least two ways.

The first way is that it is not a fully accurate representation of Judaism at the time of Jesus. The person who poses the question to Jesus was a Pharisee, as were many of the people listening to the answer. The Pharisees took the Torah, the five books of the Bible that make up the law, terribly seriously but they also applied the Oral Law, a body of wisdom that had emerged over the generations. The Oral Law teaches that saving a life is a priority over all other commandments.

So as they listened to Jesus they would have thought about these overly scrupulous religious leaders and said to themselves, "Of course, that's what you can expect from Sadducees." And, in their minds, they would have been anticipating the appearance of the hero of the tale, who would be, of course, a Pharisee, who would transcend the law. But as we know, Jesus is the master of the unexpected plot twist, and the element of surprise is this: not that the written law is transcended, but who does it—the Samaritan, the ancient enemy, the half-breed heretic that we all hate.

Now, the other way that I think this familiar approach is incomplete is that it limits our perspective to three of the characters—the Priest, the Levite, and the Samaritan—when in fact a number of people play a part, including an innkeeper, some thieves, and the victim. It's this last person, the one who is left abandoned and beaten on a dangerous road, that I'd like to focus on.

Imagine you are traveling and disaster strikes. You are helpless and wounded. Two people pass you by without assisting you—and it's devastating, because the first person you see is a ministry leader from your faith community. He looks over at you but decides not to stop. Then, the next person who drives by is one of your friends, but she too drives by. Can you just imagine how utterly abandoned you might feel as you were let down in a moment of tremendous need by someone you thought for sure you could depend upon? Actually, I think most of us don't even have to imagine this, because human beings are not perfect, and many of us have had an experience of being let down by someone we thought would be there for us.

On the other hand, like the beaten one in the story, many of us have an experience of being helped by someone from whom we never would have expected help—someone who was a surprising source of love or mercy or peace. I had many experiences of this sort of genuine and generous love coming from strangers in our meeting rooms. But my first vivid experience came when I was a young teen.

When I was thirteen years old, my 40-year-old father died suddenly. I come from a very big, loving, and ethnic Irish family, and everyone quickly gathered. In those early days of devastation and grief, we held a wake and a funeral Mass, and buried my father. But after a few weeks went by, I began to get the idea that I was supposed to be getting over this experience and moving on. I don't know what the truth of that is, whether there were subtle messages to that effect or it was just that, in my kid's perspective, I thought that. But I did think that: I should be getting over this. And I wasn't.

Right around that time, my friend Barbara asked if I wanted to go to temple with her family on Yom Kippur. I was really interested in this, and my Vatican-II-influenced mother was very supportive so I went to the synagogue with the Rosens.

About midway through the service, the Rabbi said to the congregation, "I would like everyone who has experienced the death of a loved one in this past year to stand now as we pray the *Kaddish*." Barbara leaned over and whispered to me,

"You should stand up now." And I was frozen. I whispered back to her, "I don't think I should." After all, I was a Catholic, some sort of interloper in this experience.

Without missing a beat, and with a kind of simultaneity that I marvel at to this day, Barbara who was seated at my right took one elbow and her brother Larry, who was seated at my left took the other elbow and they stood me up. And they stood alongside me as I wept and heard the community praise the name of God. The *Kaddish* ends with the words: *He who makes peace in his high holy places, may he bring peace upon us.* The congregation spoke this prayer in Hebrew but even though I didn't speak a word of Hebrew, I knew what it meant; I knew because in that moment I was overcome with the healing presence of God, the peace of God, and I knew that it was going to be okay again—someday, if not now—for me.

I didn't really know how beaten up and in the ditch I was, really, even at that time. I do know, today, that Barbara and Larry were my Samaritans. Like that Gospel traveler, they saw my need and they literally lifted me up in a way in which my own tribe, my own church, my own family, could not. God did not abandon me, like I thought—God just was going to take me by surprise. And Larry and Barbara were that surprising, unexpected vehicle through which the healing love of God could travel.

I see God in the form of a Higher Power taking people by surprise almost every time I sit and listen in a meeting. We may be broken, we may feel abandoned by God and cast aside, but divine love still flows to us—from human sources who can transmit healing, presence, and peace. (TV)

Standing in Faith

Even the hairs of your head have all been counted. Do not be afraid.
You are worth more than many sparrows. ■ LUKE 12:7

In every case, pain had been the price of admission into a new life.
But this admission price had purchased more than we expected.
It brought a measure of humility, which we soon discovered to be
a healer of pain. We began to fear pain less, and desire humility more
than ever. During this process of learning more about humility,
the most profound result of all was the change in our attitude toward
God...We saw we needn't always be bludgeoned and beaten into
humility. It could come quite as much from our voluntary reaching
for it as it could from unremitting suffering.

■ STEP SEVEN, *Twelve Steps and Twelve Traditions*

A while back, a lot of people were wearing t-shirts sporting
a company slogan: "No Fear." It spoke to a cultural trend: be
daring, be yourself, be controlled by no person or thing. A
number of popular reality TV shows were also based on that
same theme, like the aptly titled *Fear Factor*.

In the gospel today we heard Jesus exhort his disciples three
times about fear: Fear no one, he says. Do not be afraid. But
Jesus is not speaking in general about fear, but about fear in a
specific context, and that is the fear we all have of challenging
other people with his message. His words actually come in
the midst of a long discourse in the Gospel of Matthew about

discipleship. Jesus tells his followers what will be required of them, and it's not an easy message to hear. He makes it very clear: People are not going to like what you have to say, this message of radical love, radical justice, radical inclusion.

Fortunately, Jesus doesn't just challenge us. He also offers us powerful reassurance that the God we are called to proclaim, to proclaim loudly from the housetops, is a God that is fully present, fully with us. This is a God that knows us so well he keeps a hair count!

Not one sparrow falls to the ground without God's knowledge, he says. A better translation of the Greek text would be that "No sparrow 'lights' upon the ground without God's knowledge." It's not when the sparrow dies that God takes notice, but each time it lights and hops around. Can you imagine the immeasurable times that this happens in the life of a sparrow? And we are reminded that we are worth more than many sparrows.

We are called to this same discipleship today, and we are promised the same thing that those who walked with Jesus are promised: that the God of Jesus Christ, the God of faithfulness and fidelity, will see us, will be with us, will go before us every step of the way. So we don't have to be afraid to take what we've heard whispered and shout it from the housetops.

Still, I have to admit it's been a while since I was on the housetop.

I had a painful reminder of how carefully, how safely I share my faith when I was speaking with a friend. His name is Melkamu, and he is the pastor of an Oromo Lutheran Church. Melkamu was born in Ethiopia and was ordained during the years in which Ethiopian Christians were living under the persecution of a communist government.

We were in a circle of people sharing stories about our faith journeys. He told us stories of Christians, pastors and lay leaders, being persecuted and even killed because of their witness to Christ. Melkamu told us of churches and homes being burned to the ground. He spoke of people who were dragged from their families and taken to jails. He himself was imprisoned twice, at one point spending five years in prison for the crime of doing youth ministry among the Oromo people.

When Melkamu was done telling us these devastating stories, those of us who were listening just sat in silence. None of us had our public discipleship, the discipleship Jesus speaks of today, tested in this way. And then, Melkamu asked if we would listen to an Oromo Christian song that he had brought with him that he felt showed what this time was like for him. I was sure it would be a lament.

Instead, the song was joyful:

Nothing is wrong if I dance
It is okay if I jump
Why don't I sing a new song
And why don't I tell of his glory
Because his kindness is more than I can tell!

As I listened to those words, and the other powerful words in the song, words of praise and confidence in God's presence, I was moved to tears. The contrast was so profound: The incredible sacrifice and also the incredible joy of knowing Christ. I found myself wondering why I would ever be fearful of sharing my faith. Suddenly, risking the disapproval of others, their judgment, seemed like a very small price to pay. Suddenly, saying what might be heard as politically incorrect or weak-willed seemed like a pretty inconsequential barrier.

So where, I asked myself, would I be willing to stand in the sort of confidence and trust my friend was holding up to me? One place I thought of, of course, was in my faith community. But another place where I can witness to the power of knowing the God of my understanding is in my life in the program. While I do not promote my sect or denomination, or use the names of God from my Christian tradition, I do witness to the ways in which I feel my Higher Power shepherding, loving, guiding, supporting, and holding me in my life today. As I have watched my life unfold, one day at a time, I can see that my sparrow-like hops—forward, backward, this way and that—have happened under God's gaze.

Maybe it's time for us to drag out that old t-shirt, the one that says "No Fear," and wear it to a meeting, to Mass, in our lives. And as we hold our history and our hope, we can sing with our Oromo brothers and sisters:

> Nothing is wrong if we dance
> It is okay if we jump
> Why don't we sing a new song
> And why don't we tell of God's glory
> Whose kindness is more than we can tell!

(TV)

CONCLUSION

So ends our dance; so concludes our song. We have attempted to "tell of God's glory" as the limited human instruments that we are. Please forgive our frailty and incompleteness. We are always but beginners, both as disciples of Jesus and as recovering people.

As recovering people, we stake our recovery and our eternal lives on the belief that the only God worth worshiping, the only God worth turning our lives over to, is a *caring* God who initiates and sustains conscious contact with us, who gets right into the ditches of life with us and holds us close, giving us everything we need to thrive in whatever circumstances.

As we reread our homilies, we smile at the fact that we have been guilty of at least two homiletic bromides. The first is simply: "Every preacher is a beggar, telling other beggars where she found food." That brings back memories of the depression of the 1930s, when hoboes marked houses as places where food and shelter had been offered. Yes, we are a couple of spiritual tramps who have been given hospitality way beyond our expectation at many tables and in many homes. As a result, we determined a bibliography to be unnecessary. Virtually everything we have shared with you has been borrowed. Our list of sources is close to endless.

Second, we are also guilty of the cliché "Preach first and foremost to yourself." We have spoken to ourselves and we have shared with you simply "our experience, strength and hope." If we have touched your experience, we rejoice because now you are joining us in further writing the book. We hope we have been true to Ralph Waldo Emerson's words that "the deeper we go into our own experience, the more we unite with the experience of everyone else." Thank you for the privilege of sharing our lives, our faith, our recovery with you. We look forward to you sharing with us here or hereafter. Until then, God bless.